# Basic
# Wiring

## PRO TIPS AND SIMPLE STEPS

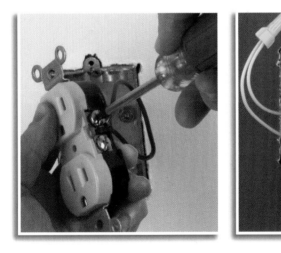

**Meredith® Books**
Des Moines, Iowa

**Stanley® Books**
**An imprint of Meredith® Books**

*Stanley Basic Wiring*
Editor: Ken Sidey
Senior Associate Design Director: Tom Wegner
Assistant Editor: Harijs Priekulis
Copy Chief: Terri Fredrickson
Managers, Book Production: Pam Kvitne,
    Marjorie J. Schenkelberg
Technical Editors, The Stanley Works: Mike Maznio, Jim Olsen
Contributing Copy Editor: Jim Stepp
Technical Proofreader: Ralph Selzer
Contributing Proofreaders: Raymond L. Kast, Steve Salato,
    Vicki Sidey, Debbie Smith
Electronic Production Coordinator: Paula Forest
Editorial and Design Assistants: Kathleen Stevens,
    Karen Schirm

**Additional Editorial Contributions from**
    **Greenleaf Publishing**
Publishing Director: Dave Toht
Writer: Steve Cory
Editorial Art Director: Jean DeVaty
Design: Rebecca Anderson
Editorial Assistant: Betony Toht
Photography: Dan Stultz, Stultz Photography
Illustrator: Dave Brandon, Art Rep Services
Technical Consultant: Joe Hansa
Indexer: Nan Badgett

**Meredith® Books**
Editor in Chief: James D. Blume
Design Director: Matt Strelecki
Managing Editor: Gregory H. Kayko
Executive Editor, Gardening and Home Improvement:
    Benjamin W. Allen
Executive Editor, Home Improvement: Larry Erickson

Director, Sales, Special Markets: Rita McMullen
Director, Sales, Premiums: Michael A. Peterson
Director, Sales, Retail: Tom Wierzbicki
Director, Book Marketing: Brad Elmitt
Director, Operations: George A. Susral
Director, Production: Douglas M. Johnston

**Meredith Publishing Group**
President, Publishing Group: Stephen M. Lacy

**Meredith Corporation**
Chairman and Chief Executive Officer: William T. Kerr

Chairman of the Executive Committee: E.T. Meredith III

All of us at Stanley® Books are dedicated to providing you with the information and ideas you need to enhance your home and garden. We welcome your comments and suggestions about this book. Write to us at:

Meredith Corporation
Stanley Books
1716 Locust St.
Des Moines, IA 50309–3023

If you would like more information on other Stanley products, call 1-800-STANLEY or visit us at: www.stanleyworks.com Stanley® and the notched rectangle around the Stanley name are registered trademarks of The Stanley Works and subsidiaries.

If you would like to purchase any of our home improvement, cooking, crafts, gardening, or home decorating and design books, check wherever quality books are sold. Or visit us at: meredithbooks.com

**Note to the Readers:** Due to differing conditions, tools, and individual skills, Meredith Corporation assumes no responsibility for any damages, injuries suffered, or losses incurred as a result of following the information published in this book. Before beginning any project, review the instructions carefully, and if any doubts or questions remain, consult local experts or authorities. Because codes and regulations vary greatly, you always should check with authorities to ensure that your project complies with all applicable local codes and regulations. Always read and observe all of the safety precautions provided by manufacturers of any tools, equipment, or supplies, and follow all accepted safety procedures.

# CONTENTS

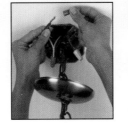

# Assembling Tools & Materials

**M**any homeowners shy away from doing their own electrical work. Not only are they afraid of shocks, they're also concerned that a mistake could result in unsafe wiring. Working with electricity is serious business, but it's within the reach of any do-it-yourselfer willing to work carefully and methodically.

### How to use this book
This book is designed to help you complete basic repairs and upgrades. It will also help you find and fix unsafe conditions that may already exist in your home.

Before you start working on any project, gain a basic knowledge of your home's electrical circuits by reading the first two chapters. Assembling Tools and Materials concentrates on how to work safely with electricity. Understanding Electrical Systems acquaints you with how a system works.

Inspecting Your Home System describes how to identify obvious defects and dangers and how to open electrical boxes to make an in-depth inspection of your home's wiring.

Mastering Skills and Techniques shows the fundamental methods for connecting wires, receptacles, switches, and fixtures.

Armed with the background from the first four chapters, you can proceed with confidence to the specific projects described in the rest of the book.

### How the projects are laid out
No two houses are exactly alike; fixtures and installations vary. If the steps depicted along the top of a page do not fit your specific situation, look below them. You'll find boxes linked to key words in the main text and others labeled "What If..." that provide additional information to help you complete a repair or upgrade.

Other features of this book include "Stanley Pro Tips," which offer tricks of the trade to help the job go smoothly. "Safety First" boxes supply important precautions to keep you safe on the job.

## A few simple skills, tools, and materials will keep you safe and productive on any wiring job.

### Chapter Preview

**Working safely**
*page 6*

**Turning off power**
*page 8*

**Tools**
*page 10*

**Materials**
*page 12*

**Make sure power is off:**
Use a voltage tester *(pages 10–11)* to confirm that the circuit you are working on is not energized.

**Catch the mess:**
An old dishrag catches plaster dust and pieces of stripped insulation. For larger jobs use a drop cloth.

**Safe tools:**
Use tools specially made for electrical work *(page 10)*.

*Most wiring chores require only a few essential tools. Invest in tools designed for electrical work (pages 10–11). They will be insulated and will strip and splice wires quickly and neatly.*

**STANLEY** PRO TIP

### When to schedule an inspection

The projects in this book—repairing and replacing devices and fixtures—typically do not require an electrical permit. However, any time you run new cable to extend a circuit and install new electrical service, you must consult with your local electrical inspector. He or she may require that you have the work inspected once or twice during the project. Follow the inspector's advice to the letter; codes vary from one city to another and between the U.S. and Canada. Remember, building codes are for your protection.

# WORKING SAFELY

**M**ost electrical work is not difficult. If you shut off the power and test to be sure it is off, you will be safe. It doesn't take a lot of time or effort to avoid a shock—just a little care and a few simple steps. Learn these steps, then make them habits.

### Never work on live wires
You may be tempted to save a trip to the service panel by connecting wires that are still live. Don't; it's not worth the risk. Always respect electrical power. Even if you have survived one shock, the next one could be more serious.

### Handle wires as if they are live
Even after you have checked and rechecked that the power is off, work as if each wire is live. That means you should never touch two wires at once, or a wire and a ground at the same time, or the bare end of a wire (except with an insulated tool). As an added precaution, lightly twist a wire nut on the bare end of any wire that you are not working on.

### Redundant protection
Most professional electricians take the extra time and trouble to provide themselves with double—even triple—protection. In addition to shutting off power and testing to make sure power is off, they wear rubber-soled shoes and use tools with rubber grips specifically designed for electrical work.

### Maintain concentration
It takes only one little lapse of concentration to create a dangerous situation. Eliminate all possible distractions. Keep nonworkers (especially children) away from the work site. Don't even play the radio while you work. Check and recheck your connections before restoring power. Give yourself plenty of time to finish a job. If you need to leave a job and pick it up again the next day, start at square one: **make sure the circuit is shut off and test for power** before proceeding.

### How circuits work:
For more information see *pages 16–17*. To learn how to check overloaded circuits, see *pages 30–31*.

## Making sure there is no power

**1** **Shut off power to the circuit.** (For more on how to shut off circuits, see *pages 8-9*). This is easy if your circuits are indexed. If they aren't, take the time to index them *(pages 48-49)*.

**2** **Test to make sure power is off** in the device using a voltage tester *(page 11)*. Insert the probes of the tester into the slotted holes of a receptacle, or touch the probes to a colored and a white wire, or to a wire and a metal box.

**STANLEY** PRO TIP

### Cut with care

Use caution any time you cut into a wall or ceiling; an electrical cable may lie behind the surface. Use a voltage detector to **check if live wires are present** *(page 11)*. Another way to check is to drill a hole in the wall or ceiling and insert a bent wire to feel for a cable. Still, you may miss a cable. To be safe, cut with a handsaw, not a power tool. Stop if you feel any resistance; it might be a cable.

**VOLTAGE TESTER**
### Test all the wires

You may find several pairs of wires in an electrical box. This indicates that more than one electrical circuit may be present. In that case, **even when you shut off one circuit, some of the wires in the box may still be hot.** Extra care is needed. Shut off the circuit you plan to work on at the service panel, open the box, then carefully remove the wire nuts and **test all the wires in the box for power.**

# Use safe tools and equipment

**3** Make sure that no one will turn on the power while you are working. Tape a note to the service panel door. You may even want to lock the panel.

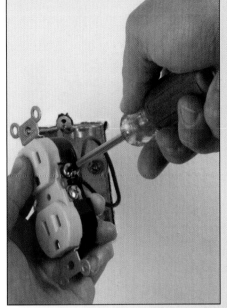

**1** Use hand tools specifically designed for electrical work. They have rubber grips that protect you from shock. Be wary of using plastic- or wood-handled tools; they may develop hairline cracks that allow electricity to arc into your hand.

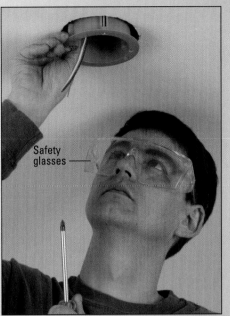

**2** Wear safety glasses anytime you might get dust, metal pieces or other material in your eyes. Wear protective clothing and rubber-soled shoes. Remove all jewelry, including a wristwatch. Don't wear loose garments that may get tangled on wires.

## SAFETY FIRST
## Know how to avoid shocks

Shocks occur because electric current always seeks to complete its circuit through the path of least resistance, and your body conducts electricity.

**You become a pathway to the ground.** If you touch only a hot wire (usually black or colored), current passes through you and to the ground. Wearing rubber-soled shoes and/or standing on a nonconducting surface (such as a wood floor) breaks the path and greatly reduces or eliminates the risk of shock.

**You become part of the circuit.** If you touch both a hot wire and a neutral wire (white) or a ground wire (green or bare copper) at the same time, current passes through you as part of the circuit. Avoid touching any bare wire; use rubber grip tools and hold them only by the handle.

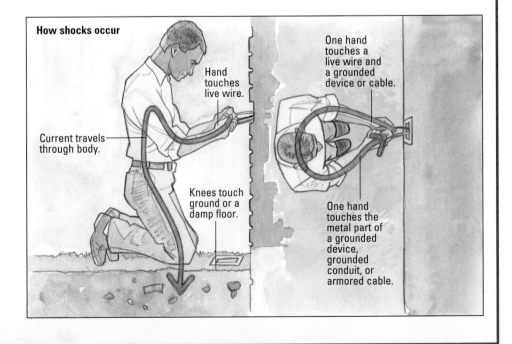

# TURNING OFF POWER

Every electrical project must start with an extremely important safety measure—the wires and devices you work on must be de-energized. Follow the steps on these pages to make sure the power to your home circuits has been turned off.

The information here will also let you know what to do when some receptacles or lights suddenly go dead, indicating that a circuit has overloaded. The place to begin is the electrical service panel.

### Accessing the service panel

A home's main service panel, which contains circuit breakers or fuses, is usually located in a utility area, easily reached but away from daily traffic flow in the house. It may be in a garage, in a basement, or (in warm climates) on the outside of the house. Unless it has been painted, the service panel will probably be a gray metal box. If you live in an apartment or condo, it may be recessed into the wall of a closet or laundry area.

You may find more than one service panel in your home. Especially in older homes, subpanels sometimes contain fuses or breakers that control power to part of the house. De-energize these just as you would a fuse or breaker in a main service panel.

You may need to get at the panel in the dark or in a hurry during an emergency. Keep the path to the panel clear; don't lean things against it, and make sure all adults in your home know where to find it.

To access the fuses or breakers inside, you probably need only to open the panel door. **If the panel appears damaged or if bare wires are visible, call a professional electrician** to repair or replace it.

**Need more help?** If you have trouble locating the service panel, **check** *pages 20–21*. If you still can't locate it, or if you are confused about how to shut it off, call an electrician.

## Breaker box

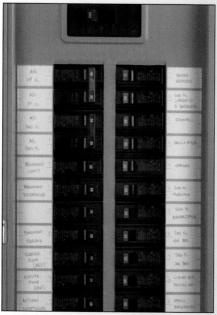

**1** After opening the service panel door, you will find rows of individual circuit breakers, which look like toggle switches, and a main breaker on top. An index indicates which parts of the house each breaker controls. (If your panel does not have an index, see *pages 48–49*.)

**2** The index should identify which breaker controls the receptacle or fixture you want to de-energize. To shut off an individual breaker, flip the switch to the OFF position. **Test the device to make sure power is off** before working on it. See *page 42* to learn how to test devices.

### CIRCUIT BREAKERS
## Two other types of breakers

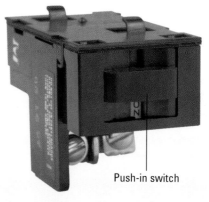

Toggle switch

Push-in switch

Breakers vary in the way they shut off when they sense an overload. One toggle type (left) has a red button that pops up when the breaker has tripped. Reactivate it by turning the switch back on. Some toggles turn partway off when they blow. To restore power, flip the switch all the way off, then on. To reset a breaker with a push-in switch (right), push on the switch to turn off power or to restore power.

**3** To turn off power to the entire house, flip off the main breaker, usually a double-wide switch located at the top of the service panel. You may want to have a flashlight handy when you turn off power.

# Fuse box

**1** If you have a fuse box, shut off power by unscrewing and removing a fuse. If there is no index telling which fuse you need to remove, see *pages 48–49.* **Test the device to make sure the power is off** *(page 42)* before doing any work. If a fuse has blown, replace it with a new one.

**2** To turn off power to the entire house, pull the main fuse block, which looks like a rectangular block with a handle. It is usually located at the top of the panel. Tug hard and straight out on the handle. **Use caution.** If you have just removed the block, its **metal parts may be hot.**

---

**SAFETY FIRST**
**Hands off live wires!**

**When turning off or restoring power in a service panel, take care not to touch any wires.** Open only the door: Do not remove the inner cover that hides the wires. (See *pages 30–31* if you need to open the cover.) Touch only the breaker. For added safety, wear rubber-soled shoes. If the floor near the box is wet, lay down a dry board and stand on it.

   **Never touch the thick wires that enter the service panel from outside the home.** They are always energized, even if the main breaker is turned off.

**WHAT IF ...**
**A fuse blows often?**

When a fuse blows often, it's tempting to replace it with one of a greater amperage. This is a dangerous mistake—house wires could burn up before the fuse blows. Check the wire gauge used in the circuit to make sure the fuse rating is correct *(pages 30-31).* A 15-amp circuit should have 14-gauge or larger wire; a 20-amp circuit, 12-gauge or larger; and a 30-amp circuit, 10-gauge or larger.

   Checking the wire gauge is easy if you have nonmetallic cable running into the box. Examine the sheathing for a stamped or printed identification which will include the gauge *(page 35).* With armored sheathing or conduit, open a receptacle on the circuit *(pages 32–33).* Check the insulation on the wires for a gauge listing or compare with a wire of known gauge.

**MAIN FUSE BLOCK**
**Check the fuses inside**

Cartridge fuses are found inside a fuse block, which is used as a main block or as a 240-volt circuit. Remove an individual cartridge fuse by pulling its blades out from holders. Test the fuse *(page 43)* and, if necessary, replace it.

# TOOLS FOR REPAIRS AND BASIC INSTALLATIONS

The tools shown here are all you need to perform the jobs in this book, as well as most other electrical projects. You can probably purchase them all for under $100.

**Tools for stripping, cutting, and joining**
A pair of **combination strippers** lets you remove insulation quickly without damaging the wire. Always use strippers—never use a knife, which can nick wires and is more dangerous to handle. The kind of wire

stripper shown below makes it easy to work in tight places. Other types of combination strippers *(page 44)* have the stripping holes nearer to the handle. They are good for general-purpose work but are difficult to use in close quarters.

With a pair of **linesman's pliers,** you can quickly and neatly twist wires together and then snip off the ends. **Side cutters,** as well as a similar cutting tool known as **diagonal cutters,** cut wires more accurately than

linesman's pliers and are easier to use in tight places. Use **long-nose pliers** to twist a wire end into a loop that fits around a terminal screw.

**Screwdrivers**
Purchase a set of **rubber-gripped screwdrivers**—both slot and phillips types. (Plastic handles can crack, opening a route for electricity to arc.) You will normally use a screwdriver with a 4- or 5-inch shank.

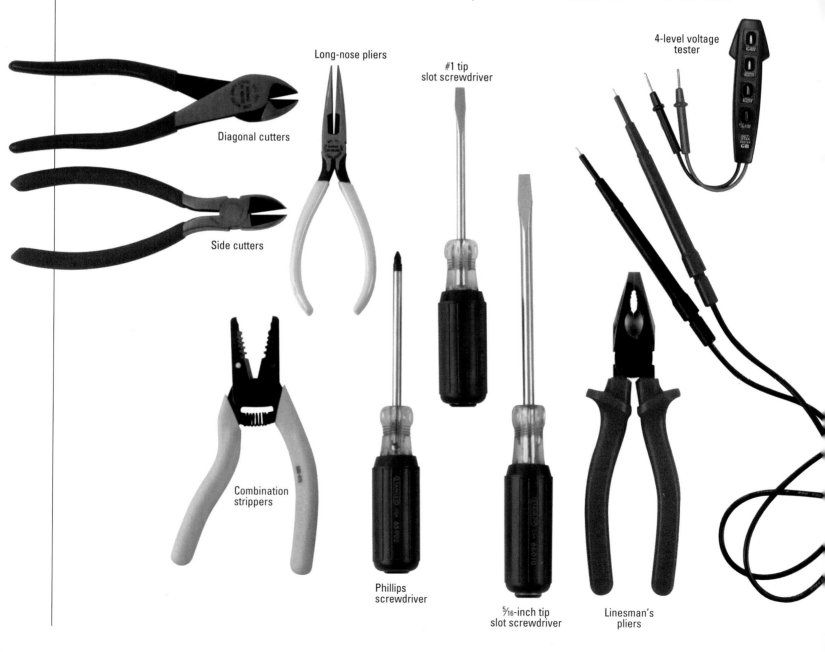

Diagonal cutters

Side cutters

Long-nose pliers

#1 tip
slot screwdriver

4-level voltage
tester

Combination
strippers

Phillips
screwdriver

⁵⁄₁₆-inch tip
slot screwdriver

Linesman's
pliers

### Testers

A **voltage tester** tells you if power is present. This is a simple but extremely important test, so spend a little extra for a reliable tester. Avoid the inexpensive, single-bulb neon testers—they burn out easily. Buy the 4-level tester or the voltage/continuity tester shown. Place the probes into the slots of a receptacle or onto terminals or bare wires to test for current.

A **voltage detector** is even easier to use: Just point it at a device, fixture, cable, or electrical box and push the button to find whether power lurks inside.

All homeowners, even those who never do electrical work, should have a **receptacle analyzer.** When plugged in, it shows whether a receptacle is wired correctly. The model shown (*below left*) tests standard and ground fault circuit interrupter (GFCI) receptacles—making it worth the slightly

higher cost. Use a **continuity tester** to check a lamp, light fixture, switch, or fuse.

### Other tools

You will sometimes need carpentry tools, such as a hammer, saw, and drill, as well as a small flashlight. If you plan to replace a houseful of devices, consider buying an electrician's tool pouch to keep tools and supplies within easy reach.

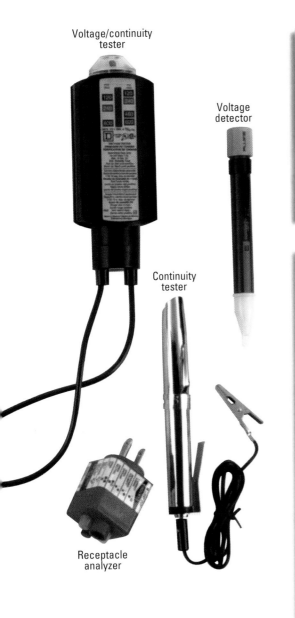

Voltage/continuity tester

Voltage detector

Continuity tester

Receptacle analyzer

**STANLEY** PRO TIP: **Tools that perform**

Generally if you buy more expensive tools labeled "professional grade," you will get reliable tools that handle well, cut cleanly, and are a pleasure to use. Examine the tools for quality before buying. Hold a pair of linesman's pliers or long-nose pliers up to a light and check the jaws as you squeeze together: the two tips should meet cleanly, and the cutting portion

should block out all light. Check screwdriver tips for nicks, and look for an indication of durability, such as "drop forged" written on the shaft. Test strippers on pieces of wire to make sure they strip insulation with ease and leave no nicks on the wire. See *page 44* for more information on using a stripper.

## Special tools that speed the job

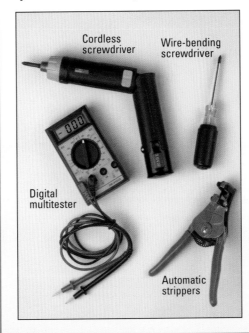

Cordless screwdriver

Wire-bending screwdriver

Digital multitester

Automatic strippers

These optional tools can lighten your workload and are worth the investment if you are doing a lot of electrical repairs.

A cordless screwdriver tightens and removes screws quickly and effortlessly. A wire-bending screwdriver easily twists wire ends into loops that fit neatly around terminal screws.

A digital multitester (preferable to an analog multitester, which has a needle and dial) performs the tasks of both a voltage tester and a continuity tester, and is needed for many repairs to appliances.

Automatic strippers are easier to use than combination strippers—you don't have to search for the correct hole every time you use them.

# MATERIALS

**Y**ou will have little trouble finding the parts you need for the projects in this book. Virtually any switch or 120-volt receptacle will fit into your electrical boxes, no matter how old your home.

When you purchase a light fixture or fan, open the box to make sure it has all the hardware necessary to mount it to your ceiling box. (See Lights and Fans, *starting on page 80,* for more on ceiling fixtures.)

At one time, it was common to wrap wire splices with several windings of cloth tape (called friction tape). Today, electrical safety codes require that all splices be capped with plastic wire nuts. As an added safety feature, many electricians wrap the wire nut and wire with electrical tape.

None of the materials shown here is expensive, so keep plenty of each in stock to save yourself shopping trips. In particular, maintain a collection of wire nuts to splice different numbers and gauges of wires.

For information on wire and cable types, see *page 35.*

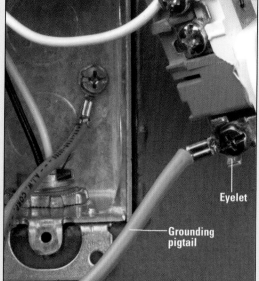

Inexpensive tape can be brittle and adhere poorly

More expensive tape is more flexible and stickier

*You may find a large bin of inexpensive electrician's tape at a hardware store or home center (above left). The cheap stuff will do the job, but you're better off spending a little more for professional-grade tape (above right). It's more flexible and stickier for more reliable coverage.*

**STANLEY** PRO TIP: **Making secure grounds**

If you have metal electrical boxes, the best way to ground devices and fixtures is by screwing a grounding wire to the box. If your wiring is not already grounded in this way, buy some small green grounding screws, made to fit in a threaded hole in the box. Use them to firmly attach the ground wire to the box.

A grounding pigtail is often easier to connect than a standard ground wire. Because it is made with stranded wire, it flexes easily and has an eyelet at each end.

For more on grounding, see *page 38.*

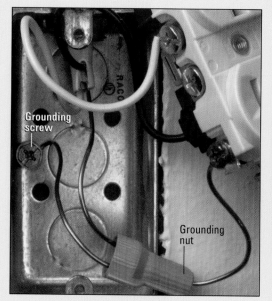

Grounding screw

Grounding nut

Eyelet

Grounding pigtail

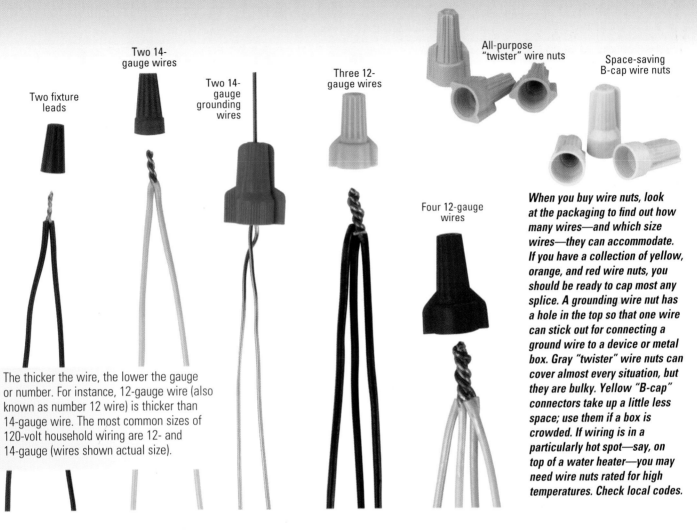

Two fixture leads

Two 14-gauge wires

Two 14-gauge grounding wires

Three 12-gauge wires

Four 12-gauge wires

All-purpose "twister" wire nuts

Space-saving B-cap wire nuts

The thicker the wire, the lower the gauge or number. For instance, 12-gauge wire (also known as number 12 wire) is thicker than 14-gauge wire. The most common sizes of 120-volt household wiring are 12- and 14-gauge (wires shown actual size).

*When you buy wire nuts, look at the packaging to find out how many wires—and which size wires—they can accommodate. If you have a collection of yellow, orange, and red wire nuts, you should be ready to cap most any splice. A grounding wire nut has a hole in the top so that one wire can stick out for connecting a ground wire to a device or metal box. Gray "twister" wire nuts can cover almost every situation, but they are bulky. Yellow "B-cap" connectors take up a little less space; use them if a box is crowded. If wiring is in a particularly hot spot—say, on top of a water heater—you may need wire nuts rated for high temperatures. Check local codes.*

## Anchoring cable and conduit

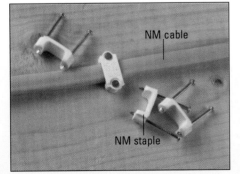

NM cable

NM staple

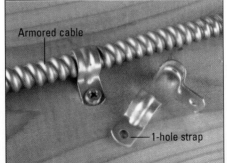

Armored cable

1-hole strap

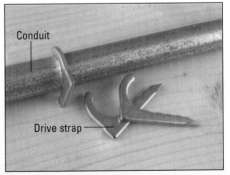

Conduit

Drive strap

Any exposed electrical cable—in a utility room, a basement, or a garage—must be firmly attached to a wall or framing.

To support sagging nonmetallic (NM) cable, purchase plastic staples made for various sizes

of cable. Hold a staple over the cable, making sure the nails are on each side of the cable, and pound in the nails. Don't damage the wire.

Attach flexible armored cable using one- or two-hole straps. Hold the strap in place and

drive a screw through the hole.

Anchor conduit by hammering a metal drive strap just beneath or beside it so that the strap's hook grabs the conduit. One- or two-hole straps and screws can also be used.

# UNDERSTANDING ELECTRICAL SYSTEMS

You should never feel that you are exploring uncharted territory when doing electrical work. Take time to become familiar with your electrical system first, before you begin any project. If you are in doubt about what to do, don't start until you are sure.

This chapter will help you understand your home's wiring, and you won't need to handle a single tool. Beginning with an overview of residential wiring, it guides you through the elements of the electrical system you'll find in your own home.

## The knowledge you need

In this chapter, you'll learn:
■ How to test for power and make sure power is off

■ How circuits work, and which parts of your house are protected by each fuse or circuit breaker in the service panel
■ How switches and receptacles work
■ How your total system is grounded
■ How each electrical box is grounded
■ How a ground fault circuit interrupter (GFCI) receptacle works, and how to make sure it is protecting you
■ How to determine the purpose and function of any wire you may encounter.

## A surface inspection

Most electrical problems are easy to spot once you know what to look for. You'll be able to see many problems without removing a cover plate or fixture. The inspection described in this chapter

will help you find and correct the dangerous situations and electrical code violations commonly found around a home.

## Getting more information

This book covers the common situations encountered in home wiring. If your house has some unusual installations, seek additional advice. You might find help at a home center or hardware store. Or call your local building department and ask for an appointment with an electrical inspector. Or you could hire an electrician to look things over and do whatever work is needed to correct the problems.

## Take time to evaluate the overall safety of your household electrical system.

## CHAPTER PREVIEW

**Understanding circuits**
*page 16*

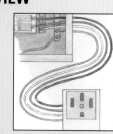

**How circuits are grounded, polarized**
*page 18*

**The house ground**
*page 19*

**Service entrance and meter**
*page 20*

**Knob and tube wiring:**
This older system uses two separate wires, rather than a cable, and passes them through porcelain knobs and tubes. It is not unsafe as long as the wires are undisturbed. However, it is ungrounded.

**Armored cable:**
Two or more insulated wires, and perhaps a ground wire, are encased in flexible metal sheathing.

**NM cable:**
Nonmetallic (NM) cable contains two or more insulated wires, plus a bare ground wire, wrapped in plastic sheathing.

*If an older home has been remodeled several times, various types of cable may exist in one electrical system. As shown above, vintage knob-and-tube wiring, **NM** cable, and armored cable enter the same electrical box.*

**Receptacles**
*page 22*

**Switches**
*page 23*

# UNDERSTANDING CIRCUITS

Electricity moves efficiently when it is flowing through a metal conductor, such as a wire or the metal insides of a switch or receptacle. Electrical current must move in a loop, or circuit. If the circuit is broken at any point, the flow of power stops.

## From power grid to service panel

Power comes to a home through the power company's thick wires, passes through a meter, and enters a service panel. The service panel parcels the power out to individual circuits, called branch circuits.

Each circuit supplies power to a number of outlets. An outlet is any place where power leaves the wires to provide service. Devices (receptacles and switches), ceiling lights and fans, and appliances (such as a water heater or a dishwasher) are the most common outlets.

## Circuit wiring

Power leaves the service panel via a "hot" (energized) wire—usually coated with insulation that is black, red, or a color other than green—and returns to the panel via a neutral wire—usually a wire with white insulation.

Another wire, typically bare or with green insulation, provides the ground. (For more about grounding, see *page 18*.)

The thicker the wire, the more electrical power it can safely carry. If too much power passes through a wire, the wire will overheat, the insulation will melt, and a fire or shock could result. The service panel (often called the fuse box or breaker box) provides protection against this possibility.

Power lines enter the service panel and energize two strips of metal called bus bars. Circuit breakers or fuses attach to the hot bus bars. Power must pass through a breaker or fuse before it leaves the service

panel and goes into the house through a branch circuit.

## Breakers and fuses

A breaker or fuse is a safety device. When it senses that its circuit is using too much power, it automatically shuts off. A breaker "trips" and can be reset; a fuse "blows" and must be replaced. Both devices keep wires from overheating.

## Volts

Voltage, measured in volts, is the amount of force exerted by the power source. Wires from the power company, as well as wires in a house, carry 120 volts. (Actually, voltage varies constantly but stays within an acceptable range, from 115 to 125 volts.)

Most outlets use 120 volts, which is provided by one hot wire bringing the power to the outlet, with one neutral wire carrying it back to the service panel. Some heavy-duty appliances, such as large air conditioners, electric ranges, and electric water heaters, use 240 volts. This power is

supplied by two 120-volt hot wires connected to the outlet or appliance, with one neutral wire.

## Amps and watts

Though the force running through all wires is the same—120 volts—different fixtures and appliances use varying amounts of power. Amperes (commonly called amps) refer to the carrying capacity of the wire. Wattage refers to the amount of power an electrical device consumes. The thicker the wire in a circuit, the more amps it can handle; the thicker the wire in a fixture or appliance, the more watts it uses. For example, a 100-watt bulb contains slightly thicker wires and uses more power than a 75-watt bulb.

The thinner a wire is, the fewer amps it can handle before it starts to overheat. That is why, for example, a circuit will overload (causing a breaker to trip or a fuse to blow) when you plug a toaster, microwave, and radio into its receptacles and use them all at the same time.

## Terms you may hear inspectors and electricians use:

**Device** refers to any electrical receptacle or switch.

**Feeder** refers to an incoming hot wire. On a ground fault circuit interrupter (GFCI) receptacle, the word "line" refers to the incoming feeder and neutral wires.

**Conductor** is basically another word for a wire.

**Outlet** is any place where electricity leaves the wiring to be used, including fixtures, receptacles, and appliances.

**Receptacle** is a device with holes, into which you can insert a plug to deliver power to an appliance, power tool, or lamp.

**Service panels:**
Panels have varying styles of covers and different styles of breakers. See *pages 30–31* for more information.

**Bus bars:**
For more about bus bars and the inner workings of service panels, see *page 31*.

**Avoid overloads:**
For more about how to avoid overloading household circuits, see *page 53*.

*The wiring plan of this kitchen and utility area demonstrates the variety of circuits found in a house. All the circuits receive power from the service head, which brings two 120-volt lines and a neutral line through the electric meter and into the service panel. The service panel in turn distributes the power. Most circuits carry 120 volts and serve receptacles, light fixtures, and moderate-demand appliances. An electric water heater requires its own 240-volt circuit, fed by doubling up 120-volt lines.*

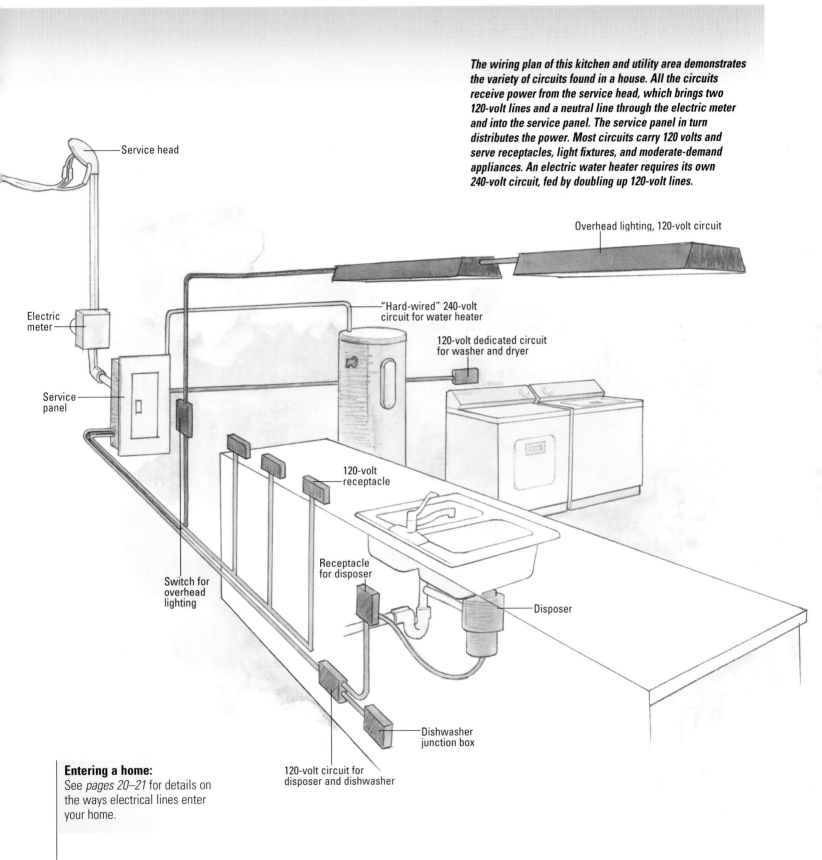

Service head

Overhead lighting, 120-volt circuit

Electric meter

"Hard-wired" 240-volt circuit for water heater

120-volt dedicated circuit for washer and dryer

Service panel

120-volt receptacle

Switch for overhead lighting

Receptacle for disposer

Disposer

Dishwasher junction box

**Entering a home:**
See *pages 20–21* for details on the ways electrical lines enter your home.

120-volt circuit for disposer and dishwasher

# HOW CIRCUITS ARE GROUNDED AND POLARIZED

If an electrical system works correctly, power travels safely through insulated wires, fixtures, and appliances. However if a receptacle suffers damage or a wire comes loose, power may flow to unwanted places, such as a metal electrical box or the metal housing of an appliance. Because the human body is a fairly good conductor of electricity, a person touching these objects will receive a painful shock. Grounding and polarization reduce this danger.

You can quickly find out whether a receptacle is grounded and polarized by using a receptacle analyzer *(page 26)*.

## Grounding

Electricity always travels the path of least resistance, either in a circuit back to its place of origin or toward the earth. A grounded electrical system provides an alternate path for the power to follow in case something goes wrong.

Many homes built prior to World War II have 120-volt circuits with only two wires and 240-volt circuits with only three wires, and no metal sheathing or conduit to act as a ground. These homes are not grounded, and receptacles in them should have only two slot-shaped holes.

Most modern homes are grounded. They have a third (or fourth) wire, usually bare copper or green insulated, called a ground wire; or their wires may run through metal conduit or flexible metal sheathing that can be used as a path for ground. A ground wire or metal sheathing carries misguided electricity harmlessly to the earth. Receptacles in these homes should have a third, round hole, which connects to the ground wire or sheathing.

## Polarization

Most receptacles—grounded or ungrounded—have one slot that is longer than the other, so that a plug that has one prong wider than the other can be inserted only one way. These receptacles and plugs are polarized.

If a polarized receptacle is wired correctly, the narrow slot connects to the hot wire (delivering power to the receptacle) and the wide slot connects to the neutral wire (carrying power back to the service panel). When you plug a light or appliance into the receptacle, its switch controls the hot wire. If the receptacle or plug is not polarized, or if a receptacle is wired incorrectly, the switch will control the neutral wire—meaning that power will still be present in the wires inside the light or appliance when you turn it off, posing a safety hazard.

**120-Volt Light Circuit**

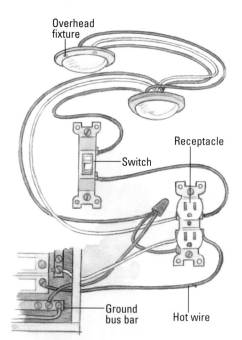

*Any circuit that includes lights should be protected by a 15-amp breaker or fuse. (A light fixture's wires are thin and may burn up before they trip a 20-amp breaker.)*

**120-Volt Receptacle Circuit**

*A receptacle circuit may be 15- or 20-amp. Black wires carry power to the receptacles, and white wires lead back to the service panel.*

**Armored cable:** Some codes do not allow use of armored cable as a ground. Check before you install.

**240-Volt Circuit**

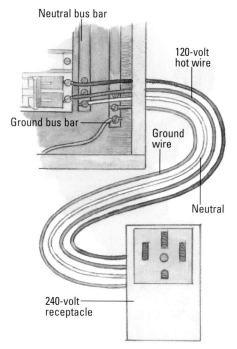

*A 120/240-volt circuit supplies power to a heavy user of power, such as an electric range or dryer. Two hot wires bring power, and one neutral leads back to the service panel. Recent codes call for a fourth ground wire.*

# THE HOUSE GROUND

**G**round wires for individual branch circuits (or metal sheathing that acts as a ground) lead back to the neutral or ground bar of the service panel. The service panel itself must be connected to the earth, so that the entire electrical system is safely grounded.

Usually, a service panel is grounded by a thick wire—bare copper or green insulated—leading to a ground rod or to a cold-water pipe. Follow the ground wire from the service panel to find how it is attached to the earth.

### Ground rod
A ground rod, made of thick copper, is driven at least 8 feet into the ground. Its top may be visible, or it may be sunk beneath the ground. It is important that the house ground wire be firmly attached to the ground rod. The connection may be a weld, or a special toothed clamp may attach the wire to the rod. Recent building codes often call for two or more ground rods, for added security.

### Cold-water pipe
The house ground wire may lead to a cold-water pipe, which in turn is connected to supply pipes that lead deep underground. The connection must be firmly clamped.

### Other methods
In rocky areas, where it is difficult to drive a ground rod 8 feet down, a grounding plate may be used. This is a thick piece of metal that is buried underneath a footing or foundation. Or, a ground wire may connect to a metal reinforcing rod embedded in a house's concrete foundation.

If you have any doubts about your home's grounding—and especially if a receptacle analyzer shows that the receptacles are not grounded—consult with a professional electrician.

**Ground rod:** Many ground lines are clamped to an 8-foot-long copper rod pounded into the ground. Often the connection is above ground *(above),* but it may be a few inches beneath.

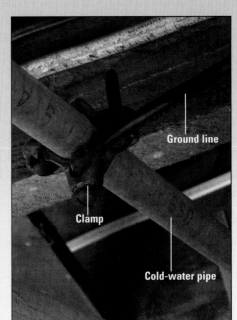

**Cold water pipes:** Because municipal water pipes lead far underground, a firm cold-water-pipe connection forms an effective ground.

## WHAT IF...
### Your house is ungrounded?

If your home's receptacles have only two holes, or if a receptacle analyzer indicates that they are ungrounded, don't panic—people have lived with ungrounded homes for decades. However, grounding considerably improves a home's safety and is well worth adding.

If you want to ground an entire system, you'll have to call in a pro to rewire the entire home—an expensive job. If you want to ground only one receptacle, ask an electrician to run an individual ground wire from the receptacle to a cold-water pipe.

Here's a simpler solution: Install ground fault circuit interrupter (GFCI) receptacles. These offer protection similar to grounding. Installed correctly, a single GFCI can protect all the receptacles on a circuit. (For more on GFCIs, see *page 76.*)

**STANLEY** PRO TIP

### Add a meter jumper

If your house ground connects to a cold-water pipe, the pipe must connect directly to municipal pipes underground. A newer water meter or a water filter may have nonmetal parts and break the connection. Clamp a copper jumper cable to either side of any such obstruction to complete the connection.

# SERVICE ENTRANCE AND METER

A power company generates electrical power and sends it to your neighborhood through overhead or underground wires. Transformers, located on utility poles or on the ground, reduce the voltage before electricity enters a home.

Power arrives at most homes via two insulated hot wires, each carrying 120 volts, plus a bare neutral wire. A pre-World War II-era home may have only one hot wire, which will provide only limited service possibilities. It should be upgraded; contact your local power company.

A service entrance consists of several parts: the wires leading from the transformer to the house (overhead wires are sometimes referred to as a service drop), the point of attachment for those wires to the house (the service head), the meter, and the wires leading from the meter to the service panel (commonly called the breaker box or fuse box).

The power company is usually responsible for the wires up to the utility splices or to the service head. A professional electrician installs the wires after the service head, as well as the meter and service panel.

With an underground service entrance, the power company brings power all the way to the meter base (see opposite page).

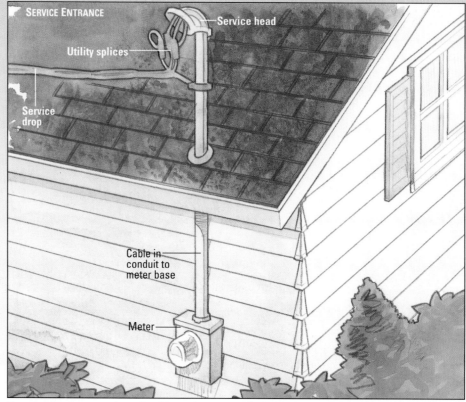

**Overhead entrance wires** should not droop lower than 12 feet from the ground at any point, and should be clear of branches, which can damage the insulation. The point of attachment and the utility splices *(below)* must be firm. The wires leading to the meter base should be protected by conduit.

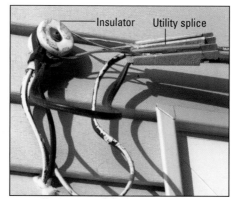

**On older homes,** the point of attachment may be a porcelain insulator, securely screwed into a framing member within the wall. Call the power company if the insulator is cracked or loose.

**A service head** (or masthead) has insulated openings with an entrance cap to keep the wires dry. Older variations have a gooseneck pipe with an opening that points downward so rainwater will not enter. On either, check that the insulation is not frayed near the opening and that the pipes are firmly anchored.

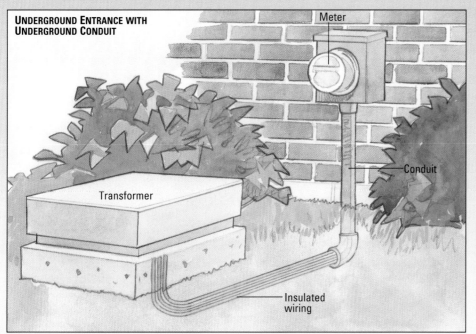

**UNDERGROUND ENTRANCE WITH UNDERGROUND CONDUIT**

Meter

Conduit

Transformer

Insulated wiring

An underground entrance begins with a transformer, usually sitting on a concrete pad. Three insulated wires, buried 3 or 4 feet underground, run to the house. These wires may be encased in conduit. When they reach the house, they extend up, through metal or PVC conduit, to reach the meter.

In some locales, the meter may be placed away from the house, near the transformer. Find out where the underground wires are located to avoid accidentally nicking them with a shovel. Call your local utility company to mark the locations before you start digging.

**Read your meter:** Even if the power company doesn't require you to read your meter, you may want to compare numbers at the beginning and end of each billing cycle to make sure the utility is charging you correctly. To read a dial meter, write down the digit that each dial is pointing to, working from left to right.

## From the meter base to the service panel

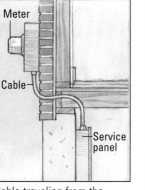

Meter

Conduit

Elbow

Service panel

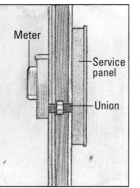

Meter

Cable

Service panel

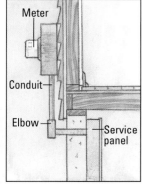

Meter

Service panel

Union

A service panel is usually located as near as possible to the meter, linked in one of the ways pictured above.

Cable traveling from the meter to the panel may be exposed, or it may be encased in conduit.

(In warm climates, the service panel may be on the outside of the house.)

# RECEPTACLES

The 120-volt duplex receptacle (a receptacle with two outlets) is the workhorse of any residential electrical system. Because household wiring has remained standardized almost from the time it was first introduced, the duplex receptacle accepts even the oldest tools and appliances.

Receptacles are easy to replace, so install new ones if your old receptacles are damaged, paint-encrusted, or simply ugly. (See *page 75* for more on how to install them.) However, do not replace an older, ungrounded receptacle with a three-hole receptacle unless you can be sure it will be grounded. (See *page 42* to test grounding.)

If the wires connecting to a receptacle are 12-gauge or thicker, and it is protected by a 20-amp circuit breaker or fuse, you can safely install a 20-amp receptacle. Otherwise, install a standard 15-amp receptacle. Amp ratings are printed or stamped on the side of the receptacle.

Some people prefer to mount the receptacle in the box with the ground hole on top; others prefer it on the bottom. In terms of safety, it does not matter. For appearance, be consistent.

Bargain-bin receptacles are fine for most purposes. But if a receptacle will receive a lot of use or is in a high-traffic area—a busy hallway, for example—purchase a "spec-rated" or "commercial" receptacle, which is stronger and more resistant to damage.

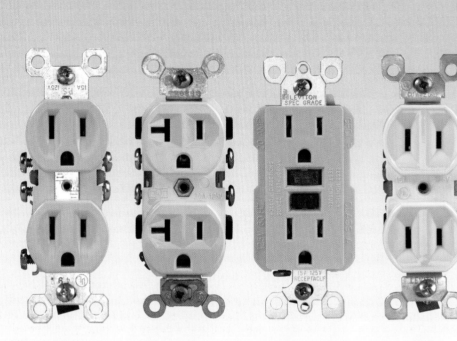

The most common electrical device in your home is probably a **grounded 15-amp, 120-volt receptacle.** It supplies adequate power for all but the most power-hungry appliances and tools.

If a receptacle's neutral slot (the longer one) has a horizontal leg, it is rated at 20 amps. Codes often call for **20-amp receptacles** in kitchens or workshops, where power use is heavy.

A **GFCI** (ground fault circuit interrupter) receptacle provides extra protection against shocks and is required by code in damp areas. (See *page 76* for more on GFCIs.)

An **ungrounded receptacle** has two slots and no grounding hole. If one slot is longer than the other, it is polarized (*page 18*).

## 240-volt receptacles

Appliances that use 240 volts are all rated for certain levels of amperage and have plugs configured to fit only one type of receptacle. Here are the common types.

A **dryer receptacle** supplies the heating element with 240 volts and the timer and buzzer with 120 volts. The receptacle shown requires four wires; older models use only three wires. (See *page 64* for how to replace a dryer cord.)

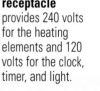

An **electric range receptacle** provides 240 volts for the heating elements and 120 volts for the clock, timer, and light.

This single-outlet **air conditioner receptacle** provides 240 volts only. Check your air conditioner to make sure its amperage and plug configuration match the receptacle.

# SWITCHES

**T**urn a switch on and it completes the circuit, letting electricity flow through it. Turn it off, and the circuit is broken; the switch creates a gap that stops the flow.

## Essential switches

The most common household switch, a single-pole, has two terminals and simply turns power on or off.

A three-way switch has three terminals; a four-way has four. These are used to control a light from two or three locations, such as in a stairwell, at either end of a hallway, or in a large room with more than one entrance.

A dimmer switch (or rheostat) controls a light's intensity. Usually you can replace any single-pole switch with a dimmer. However, buy a special fan or fluorescent dimmer switch to control a fan or a fluorescent light—a standard dimmer will overheat and can burn out a fan motor or a fluorescent tube.

## Special switches

In addition to the familiar toggle and rotary switches, specialty switches can do everything from turning on when you walk into a room to varying the speed of whole-house fans. You'll also find special-duty switches that can be time-programmed or that let you know if a remote light is on or off. Decorative switches include styles that rock back and forth or slide up and down rather than toggling. (See pages 72–73 for other switch options.)

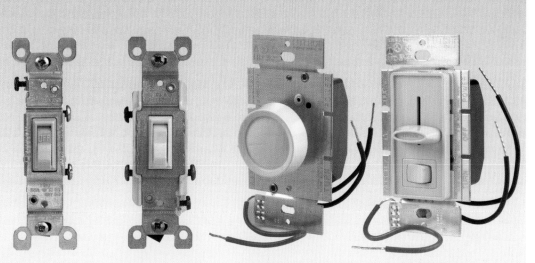

A **single-pole** switch has two terminals and a toggle labeled ON and OFF. Always connect two hot wires to it, not two neutrals.

A **three-way** switch has three terminals, and its toggle is not marked for on or off. (See page 70 for wiring instructions).

A **rotary dimmer** switch is the most common type. Some styles look like toggle switches. (See page 71 for instructions to install a dimmer switch.)

A **sliding dimmer** with an on/off toggle "remembers" how bright you left the light the last time it was on.

## Two ways to wire a switch

**End-line switch wiring:** If power goes to the fixture first and then to the switch, you have "end-line" wiring. Only one cable enters the box, coming from the fixture. Here, the white wire is taped or painted black to indicate that it is hot.

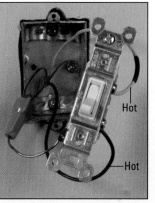

Hot

Hot

**Power through switch:** With "through wiring," power enters the switch box. The feed wire (the hot wire coming from the service panel) runs to the switch before it goes to the fixture. Two cables enter the box—one coming from power and one going to the fixture. The neutrals are spliced, and a hot wire connects to each terminal.

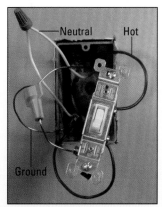

Neutral

Hot

Ground

## To ground or not to ground?

Your switches may not have a grounding screw terminal—the ground wire may travel past the switch to the light fixture. This is not unsafe, but recent building codes call for switches to be grounded.

# INSPECTING BOXES & WIRES

The previous chapter introduced the basics of how an electrical system works. Now it's time to take a closer look at your home's system and its components. This chapter shows how to perform an in-depth examination, including service panels, electrical boxes, switches, outlets, and wires.

### Turn off power

The most important safety step for these projects is to make certain that the power in your work area is turned off. If power is not off, you face serious risk of shock when you remove cover plates or open boxes. Review the information on working safely presented on *pages 6-9*.

### Meeting code requirements

Because building safety codes change over the years (they usually become stricter), wiring that was considered correct 15 years ago may not meet code requirements today. In most cases, it's okay to leave old wiring as-is, but any new wiring must meet current codes. Of course, any time you find dangerous wiring, you should correct it.

This book provides the know-how for replacing existing devices and fixtures. You probably do not need a permit or an official inspection for any of the projects in this book. But if you are puzzled by wiring you see, or are not sure whether it is safe, consult your local building department or hire a professional electrician.

### Hiring a pro

If you need to hire a professional, get bids from three or more contractors who are licensed to work in your area and are covered by liability insurance.

A contract should list in detail everything that will be installed, including the number of receptacles and switches. Ask how many holes will be cut into walls and ceilings, and if patching and painting are included in the price. Make sure the electrician—not you—is responsible for getting the permit and passing all the inspections

## Here's how to make a safe, in-depth inspection of service panels, subpanels, and junction boxes.

## CHAPTER PREVIEW

**Surface inspection**
*page 26*

**Service panels**
*page 30*

**Opening boxes**
*page 32*

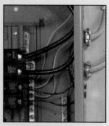

**Junction boxes and subpanels**
*page 34*

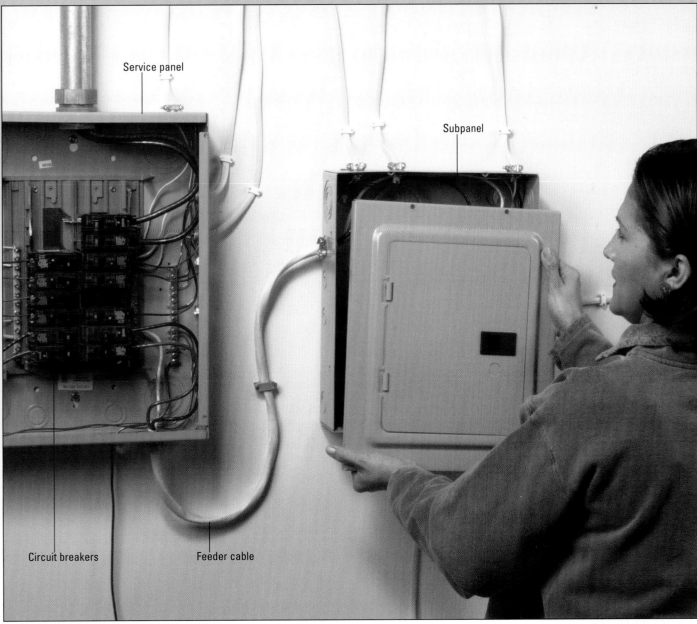

Service panel

Subpanel

Circuit breakers

Feeder cable

*A service panel may appear at first to be a jumble of wires and connectors. But after studying this chapter, you will understand what each wire and each circuit breaker does.*

**Wire, cord, and cable**
*page 35*

**Inspecting boxes**
*page 36*

**Grounding**
*page 38*

**Difficult wiring configurations**
*page 39*

# SURFACE INSPECTION

Even if your electrical system has been trouble-free for decades, it may not be completely safe. On the next four pages, you'll learn how to spot some obvious shortcomings often found in household electrical systems.

To perform this inspection, the only tools you'll need are a receptacle analyzer and a flashlight. You won't have to remove any cover plates or open any boxes, but be prepared to move furniture to uncover every outlet and device.

In addition to living areas, check in out-of-the-way places such as garages, basements, attics, utility rooms, or crawl spaces. There you may find exposed cables and electrical boxes, which will help you better understand your wiring.

## SAFETY FIRST
### Three-prong adapters are for grounded circuits only

If your home has ungrounded receptacles that lack a third hole for grounding, you may be tempted to use a three-hole adapter like this one. Be aware, however, that since the box is not grounded, the appliance or tool plugged into it will not be grounded.

## Testing receptacles

Receptacle analyzer

**Grounded and polarized:** Begin an inspection by plugging a receptacle analyzer into each outlet of every 120-volt receptacle in your home. It quickly tells whether receptacles are grounded and polarized. If only one or two receptacles lack grounding or polarizing, examine the wiring in each more closely. (See *pages 36-38* for more in-depth inspections. To wire them correctly, see *page 75*.) If all or most of the receptacles test as ungrounded, check that the house ground wire is firmly attached *(page 19)*. If you cannot solve the problem, call a professional electrician.

Test button

**GFCI:** A GFCI receptacle offers effective protection against shock, but it can wear out and lose its ability to work properly. Test the device once a month by pushing the test button. Doing so should shut off power. If it doesn't, replace the GFCI *(page 76)*.

Mounting screw

Short slot

**Two-hole receptacles:** The box still may be grounded, even if the receptacle lacks a grounding hole. Poke one probe of a voltage tester into the short slot and touch the other to the mounting screw (scrape off any paint first). If the tester glows, you can install a grounded receptacle *(page 75)*.

# Checking receptacles for damage

**Cracks:** A cracked receptacle may work just fine, but don't take a chance. The contacts on the inside could be damaged, creating sparking and shorts. Replace the receptacle *(page 75)*.

**Missing plate:** A cover plate is not just for show; it protects you from the live wires that lie just an inch or so behind the wall's surface. Install cover plates wherever they are missing.

## SAFETY FIRST
## Protecting kids from shocks

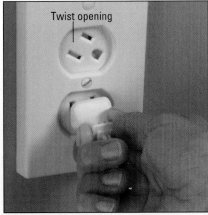

Receptacles are located at a tempting height for babies and toddlers. Protect them by pushing plastic inserts into each outlet.

For more secure protection, purchase a special cover plate with outlet covers that must be twisted before a plug can be inserted, or buy a receptacle with sliding protective covers.

# Problems with switches

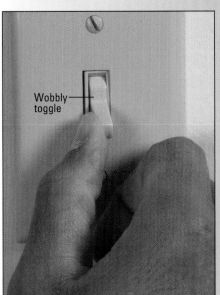

**Loose switch:** If a toggle feels loose or wobbly, **shut off power to the circuit**, remove the cover plate, and tighten its mounting screws. If it still wobbles, replace the switch *(page 69)*.

**Missing knob:** A dimmer switch missing its knob or lever is more than just an eyesore and an inconvenience; it is easily damaged. Replace the knob or install a new dimmer.

# Dangerous cords and plugs

**Overload:** This tangle of cords plugged into one receptacle places it and its circuit at risk of overloading. The cords also create a tripping hazard. A safer alternative: Install an additional receptacle or two, using surface-mounted raceway components *(pages 78–79)*.

**Cracked plug:** A cord plug protects your fingers from dangerous amounts of electricity. If a plug is damaged in any way, replace it *(page 54)*.

Cracked plug body

**Taped cord:** A repair like this is not only unsightly; it's dangerous. Tape, even if wound tightly and neatly, can come loose, and youngsters might be tempted to unwrap it. Replace the cord *(page 55)*.

# Risky wires and cables

**Loose cable:** All exposed cable should be securely anchored to minimize the risk of accidentally snagging it. Anchor the cable using staples or straps *(page 13)*. Never hang anything on exposed electrical cable.

**Exposed splices:** Safety codes strictly forbid any wire splices outside of approved electrical boxes. Exposed splices like this may come loose if bumped, causing shock or fire. Have an electrician install a junction box.

# Light fixture problems

**No cable clamp:** Anytime cable enters a metal box, it must be held firmly in place with an approved clamp. Cable that is loose like this is easily damaged by the metal box's edges. Install a clamp like the one shown on *page 37*.

**Bare bulb:** An illuminated light bulb is hot enough to ignite nearby clothing or cardboard, and it is easily broken. Install a protective globe fixture *(pages 84–85)*.

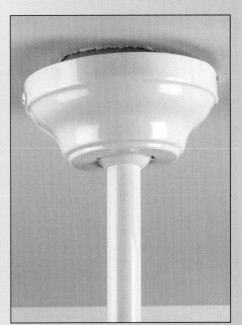

**Loose fixtures:** Sometimes a ceiling fan or a heavy chandelier will come loose and fall from the ceiling. Check that your fan is securely mounted to a fan-rated box *(pages 92–94)*.

**Old wiring:** If you find old knob-and-tube wiring like this, don't panic. If it was properly installed and is not damaged, it can be safe. Check that the insulation is not cracked and take steps to ensure that the wiring will not get bumped.

**Overheating:** When you remove a light fixture's cover to change a bulb, check for evidence of overheating. If you see a brown spot, or if the wire insulation has become brittle, replace the fixture *(pages 84–85)*.

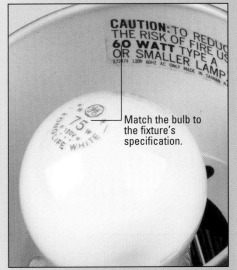

Match the bulb to the fixture's specification.

**Wrong wattage:** Heed the sticker telling you how much wattage a light fixture can handle. If you use bulbs of higher wattage, the fixture will overheat.

# SERVICE PANELS

If your home has undergone remodeling through the years, new circuits probably have been added to the service panel. Even if the panel was properly installed, mistakes may have been made later. Here's how to safely remove the cover of a service panel and inspect for damage or incorrect wiring.

### Shut off power
Before removing a cover, **shut off the main breaker or pull the main fuse** *(pages 8–9)*. This will de-energize everything in the panel except the thick wires that come from the outside and attach to the main shutoff. Those are still live, so stay away from them. Wear rubber-soled shoes and stand on a dry surface, just in case you accidentally touch a live wire.

### Check the obvious
A service panel must be kept dry, clean, and undisturbed. If you see dampness or signs of rust, find out how water is getting in and seal off any cracks or holes. If the panel is badly dented or if rust is extensive, have an electrician inspect it.

Clean away any dust, dirt, and construction debris inside the panel. They pose a fire hazard.

### Wire problems
All the wires in a service panel should run in an orderly fashion around the perimeter of the panel. They should be clear of bus bars and breakers.

Carefully inspect for any nicked or cracked wire insulation. If the damage is minor to just a few wires, you may be able to fix it yourself. See *page 65* to learn how to repair damaged wires. Call in a pro if the damage is extensive.

One wire should connect to each circuit breaker or fuse, although sometimes two wires are allowed. If you see more than two wires on any connection, call in a professional.

**Shut off power:** See *pages 8–9* for how to access and shut off power in a service panel.

## Opening the panel

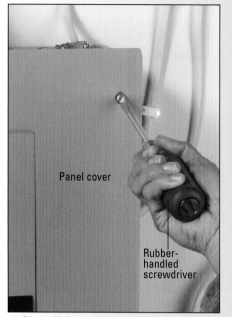

Panel cover

Rubber-handled screwdriver

**1** **Shut off the main breaker.** Locate the cover screws; placement varies according to manufacturer. Unscrew each and set them where they won't get lost.

**2** Grasp the cover at the bottom and gently pull the bottom outward. Lift up to unhook the cover at the top and remove the cover.

REMOVE THE COVER
### Opening panels with two covers

Some panels have two covers. Remove the outer cover to access all the breakers and the inner cover to access the wires.

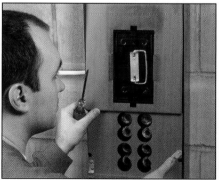

**1** Remove the mounting screws. You may have to remove a mounting screw below the cover. Lift the outer cover up and out.

**2** The inner cover has mounting screws attached to tabs. Unscrew them, then pull the inner cover off.

# Inspecting the panel

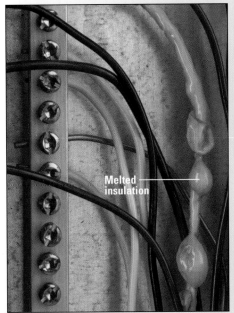

**Overheated wires:** Look for signs of overheating. If you spot a wire with melted insulation, check to see if the circuit breaker or fuse that protects it is the correct amperage. If you find obvious signs of fire, such as a charred bus bar or housing, call a professional electrician for evaluation.

**Wires too close:** If any wire comes close to an electrical connection, move the wire to the side, if possible. Don't push too hard or you may disconnect it. If things seem hopelessly tangled, call in a pro.

**Wrong amperage:** Check the wire gauge. If it is not printed on the wire's insulation, compare the wire with a known gauge—a #14 wire is thinner and belongs on a 15-amp circuit; a #12 wire is thicker for a 20-amp circuit *(page 13)*. If a breaker's amperage is too high for its circuit's wire, call a pro.

**SAFETY FIRST**
## Correct amperage of fuses

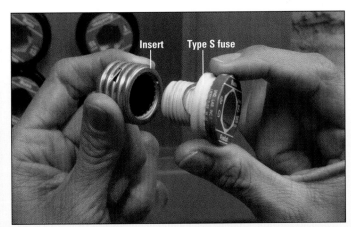

**Likely overload:** If you find a 30-amp fuse on a typical household circuit, it likely was installed by someone who got tired of changing 20- or 15-amp fuses on an overloaded circuit. This is very unsafe. Only circuits using #10 or thicker wire should be on a 30-amp circuit; smaller wires may burn up before the fuse blows.

**Inserts for safety:** To make sure no one can install an incorrectly sized fuse, use Type S fuses, which come with inserts. Once the insert is screwed into the panel, it is impossible to install a fuse of a higher amperage.

# OPENING BOXES

**S**ome homeowners fear the power that lurks behind a receptacle cover plate or light fixture. Others dive in with reckless abandon. These pages chart a middle course, preparing you to work with both confidence and caution.

**Shut off power to the circuit first** *(page 8)*. Do an initial test for power. Test a receptacle by inserting the prongs of a voltage tester into the slots of one outlet, then the other. Test a switch or light fixture by flipping on the switch. Even if the initial test indicates no power, there still might be power in the box. Use a voltage tester to double-check inside the box *(Step 2)*.

## Removal tips

Grasp a rubber-grip screwdriver only by the rubber handle when removing screws. Stand on a fiberglass or wood ladder (not aluminum) when removing an overhead light fixture.

Cover plates are cheap, so don't hesitate to replace one that is ugly or slightly damaged.

If your light fixture installation has hardware different from what is shown here, see *pages 84–86* for mounting options.

## PRESTART CHECKLIST

☐ **TIME**
A minute to open a switch or receptacle; several minutes to remove a fixture

☐ **TOOLS**
Rubber-grip #1 slot and phillips screwdrivers, voltage tester

☐ **PREP**
Spread an old dish towel or small drop cloth to catch debris when you remove receptacle cover plates. Use a sturdy fiberglass ladder for reaching ceiling fixtures.

# Receptacle and switch boxes

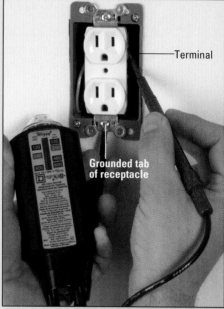
Terminal

Grounded tab of receptacle

**1** **Shut off power.** Use a small-tipped (#1) slot screwdriver to remove cover plate mounting screws. If the cover plate does not come off easily, pry it gently from the wall. If it has been painted over, cut lightly around its perimeter with a utility knife so paint won't chip when you remove it.

**2** **Test again for power**—there may be live wires in the electrical box that do not connect to the device or fixture. Touch voltage tester probes to all possible wire combinations. If you have a metal box, also test by touching one probe to the box and the other probe to each wire.

**STANLEY** PRO TIP: **What the wire colors mean**

Wire insulation colors have straightforward meanings: A black wire is hot, bringing power from the service panel to the box; a white wire is neutral, carrying power back to the panel; and a bare or green-insulated wire is the ground. Other colored wires—red is the most common—also carry power. *(See pages 16–18 for more on circuits.)* However, it is not unusual to find amateur wiring with the colors mixed up. If you suspect this is true in your house, call in a pro.

If you have old wires that all look black or gray, it may not be obvious which is hot and which is neutral. If your metal boxes are grounded, remove wire nuts and touch one probe of a voltage tester to the box. Touch the other probe to each wire in turn. The tester will glow when you touch the hot wire. If the wiring is in a receptacle box, plug in a receptacle analyzer. It will indicate a fault if the hot wire has been improperly connected to the silver terminal of the receptacle.

**Stay safe:** A voltage tester is an essential tool for electrical work. Buy one and use it.

# Opening a fixture

**3** Unscrew the screws holding the device to the box; they will come out of the holes in the box but remain attached to the device by little pieces of plastic or cardboard. Carefully grab the device by its plastic parts only and gently pull it out. Inspect the wiring and the box.

**1** **Shut off power.** Position the ladder so you can reach and see all around the light fixture. With your fingers, loosen but do not remove at least two of the setscrews that hold the globe. If a screw is rusted, you may need a screwdriver or pliers to turn it. Remove the globe.

**2** Find the screws that hold the fixture to the ceiling box (usually there are two). Unscrew them, supporting the fixture with your other hand. Gently pull the fixture down. If the fixture is heavy, support it with a coat hanger or stiff wire while you inspect the box and wiring.

## WHAT IF...
### Your house has aluminum wiring?

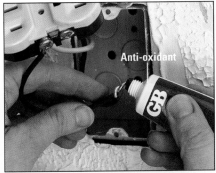

Anti-oxidant

Some houses built in the early 1970s have aluminum wiring. It is dull silver in color, thicker than copper wiring, and often has "AL" printed on its insulation.

Aluminum wiring expands and contracts with changing temperatures. Over time, it often works loose from terminals. Wherever aluminum contacts a copper terminal or wire, it will eventually oxidize, creating a bad connection. For these reasons, aluminum was banned from electrical systems a few years after builders started using it.

Don't panic if you find aluminum wiring in your house. Rewiring a house with copper is probably not necessary. Instead, make sure that all the switches and receptacles are labeled CO/ALR, meaning it is safe to wire them with aluminum. Wherever you must splice an aluminum wire with a copper lead (for example, when you install a light fixture), squirt a bit of anti-oxidant on the connection before you put on the wire nut. Anti-oxidant and CO/ALR devices are available at home centers or electrical suppliers.

## CEILING BOX
### Center-mount ceiling fixture

Some light fixtures mount via a nut and a single-threaded nipple (small pipe). Support the fixture with one hand and unscrew the nut. Then slide the fixture down and out.

# JUNCTION BOXES AND SUBPANELS

In addition to a service panel, switches, receptacles, and light fixtures, most houses have junction boxes. These are metal or plastic electrical boxes that enclose spliced wires. No electrical splice or connection should exist outside of an approved electrical box.

### Where to find junction boxes

You'll find junction boxes in utility areas, such as a garage or basement. Less commonly, they are located in living areas. A junction box is covered with a blank cover plate, usually held in place with screws, which can be removed in order to inspect the box. Most junction boxes are about 4 inches square; some are larger.

### Subpanels expand service

A subpanel holds not only wires but also circuit breakers or fuses. It is used to expand service—for instance, when an addition is built and new circuits are added. Open and inspect a subpanel the same way you would a service panel (pages 30–31).

A subpanel connects to the main service panel by a feeder cable with thick wires. A double-pole circuit breaker or a large fuse in the main service panel controls power to the subpanel. To de-energize it, shut off the "feeder breaker" or fuse in the main panel.

### Double-pole breaker:

This circuit breaker has two connected toggle switches. It connects to both hot bus bars to provide 240 volts of power. It usually provides power to a 240-volt appliance; sometimes, it supplies two 120-volt circuits.

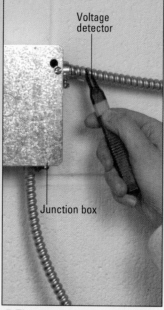

Voltage detector

Junction box

**1** The wires of more than one circuit are often in the same junction box. **Shut off power at the service panel** (page 8), then use a voltage detector (page 42) to test each cable in the box, as well as the box itself.

Junction box cover

**2** In a utility area, the blank cover will probably be metal; in a living area, you may find a plastic cover. Loosen or remove the screws and remove the cover.

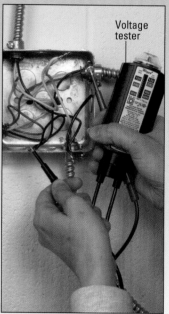

Voltage tester

**3** Double-check for power using a voltage tester (page 42) on all the wires.

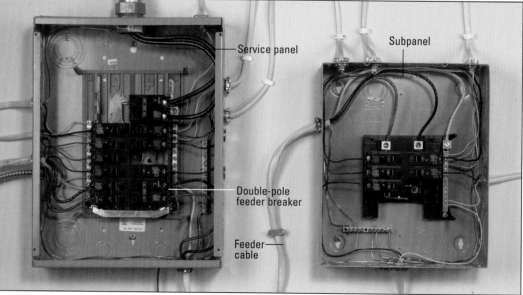

Service panel

Subpanel

Double-pole feeder breaker

Feeder cable

**Service panel and subpanel:** In a typical setup, a 30-amp or more double-pole feeder breaker in the service panel controls the power that goes to the subpanel via a feeder cable. If the main service panel is a fuse box, a fuse block containing cartridge fuses supplies power to the subpanel. The subpanel is wired much like the main panel and protects individual circuits in the same way (see pages 30–31 to remove covers).

# WIRE, CORD, AND CABLE

**M**ost house wires—the wires that run from the service panel, through walls and to electrical boxes—are solid-core, meaning they are made of a single, solid strand. Light fixtures and some switches have leads—wires made of many thin strands of thin wire, which are more flexible. The thicker a wire, the lower its number; for instance, #12 wire is thicker than #14.

*Cord,* used for appliances and electrical lights, typically has two stranded wires encased in a molded plastic insulation.

*Cable* refers to two or more wires encased in a protective sheathing. **Nonmetallic (NM) cable** has a plastic sheathing and is available in a flat profile or a round profile. Printing on NM sheathing

indicates the number and size of its wires. For instance, "14/2" means the cable contains two #14 wires, plus a bare ground wire; "12/3" indicates three #12 wires plus a ground. The forerunner to NM was **fabric-sheathed cable**, no longer sold but found in older homes.

**Armored cable** has a flexible metal sheathing. There are two types: **MC,** which carries two or three wires plus a ground wire, and older **BX,** which has no ground wire but has a thin, brittle aluminum wire running through it. **Metal conduit** is pipe through which wires are

run. (Because they are made of metal, BX and metal conduit can be used for ground, taking the place of a ground wire.)

**Underground feed (UF)** cable has sheathing that is molded to the wires to protect against moisture in outdoor installations. Telephone cable with four thin wires is increasingly being replaced by **Category 5** cable, which can carry lines for telephone, modem, and computer networking. **Coaxial** cable, used for cable TV and radio antennas, contains a single solid wire encased in sheathing that includes metal mesh.

Armored MC

Fabric-sheathed cable

Armored BX

Metal conduit

NM (round-profile)

Underground feed (UF)

Category 5

Coaxial

NM (flat-profile)

**Conduit options:** Two less common conduit options are gray plastic conduit and flexible metal conduit called Greenfield.

# INSPECTING BOXES

**O**nce you've removed a cover plate or light fixture, it takes only a few seconds to check the wiring inside for damage or unsafe connections.

**Shut off power and test to see that power is off before you touch any wires.** Use rubber-gripped tools. Often you'll need to gently pull the device out of the box to inspect it.

Always assume that the wires are hot, even though you have de-energized the circuit. Touch only wire nuts or wire insulation—never bare wires—with your fingers.

Before you replace the devices into their boxes, wrap the terminal connections with electrical tape. The added protection helps hold wires in place and keeps terminal screws from touching the sides of a metal box.

**STANLEY** PRO TIP

### Check the GFCI wiring

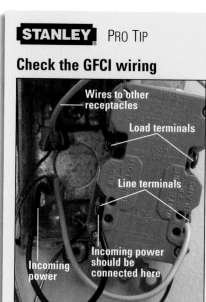

A ground fault circuit interrupter (GFCI) protects you from shock, but only if it is wired correctly. The wires coming from the power source must connect to the terminals labeled LINE. These wires will test "hot" when disconnected from the device when the circuit is live. Remember it this way—L"in"E. The wires leading out to other receptacles must connect to the LOAD terminals *(page 76)*.

## Check for incorrect wiring

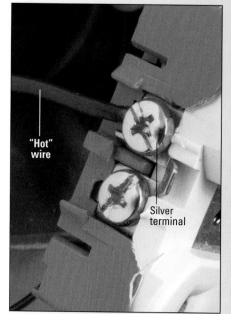

"Hot" wire — Silver terminal

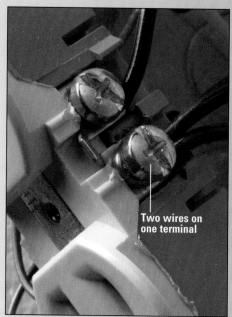

Two wires on one terminal

**Reversed connections:** The black or colored wire (hot) must be connected to a brass-colored terminal; the white wire (neutral) to the silver terminal. If the wires are reversed, the receptacle will supply power but will not be polarized *(page 18)*. Connect the wires to the correct terminals.

**Too many wires:** It is against building safety code to connect two or more wires to a single terminal, because they can easily come loose. Splice the two wires into a pigtail, and connect the pigtail to the terminal *(page 47)*.

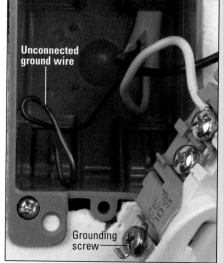

Unconnected ground wire

Grounding screw

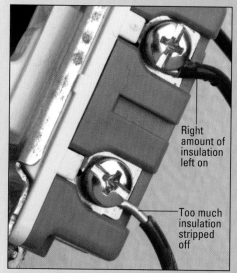

Right amount of insulation left on

Too much insulation stripped off

**No ground:** A receptacle that is not grounded delivers power but lacks an important safety feature. Connect the ground wire to the receptacle's ground screw and test with a receptacle analyzer. For other grounding methods, see *page 38*.

**Not enough insulation:** A good electrician covers as much bare wire as possible. The bottom wire has too much insulation stripped, making it unsafe. Cover it with tape. Better yet, cut, restrip, and reconnect the wire *(page 65)*.

## Check for damaged wire

**Exposed bare wire:** Even new wiring may have nicks and cuts in the insulation, leaving bare wire dangerously exposed. Wrap a small nick tightly with electrician's tape.

**Cracked insulation:** Older insulation or insulation behind an inadequately shielded fixture may become brittle and easily cracked. Seal it with shrink-wrap tubing *(page 65)*.

### NICKS AND CUTS
### Protecting wires in armored cable

If your wiring system uses armored cable, check to see that plastic bushings were installed wherever wires enter a box. Armored cable's sheathing has sharp edges, which can gouge insulation. If you don't see bushings, buy a packet of them and install them. Do this whether you see damaged insulation or not, to protect the wires from any sharp edges. Slip a bushing around the wires, then slide it down into the sheathing.

## Box problems

**Loose box:** A loose box can lead to damaged wires and a faulty connection. If the box is next to a stud, remove the cover and pull out the device. Drill a hole in the side of the box and secure it with a screw into the stud. Or replace with an "old-work" box that fastens to drywall.

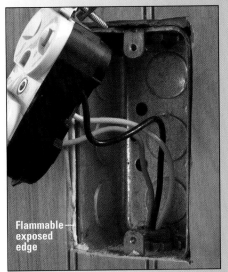

**Recessed box:** Codes call for all boxes to be nearly flush with the surrounding wall surface so wires are safely enclosed. If you have wood paneling, an improperly recessed box poses a fire danger. Install a box extender *(page 65)*.

# GROUNDING

**B**uilding codes have changed over the years, and they vary from region to region. As a result, grounding methods can vary widely. You may find any of the configurations shown here in your home.

No matter the method used, it's important that the ground circuit provides an unbroken path to the earth *(pages 18–19)*. Ground wires must be firmly connected at all points. If conduit or sheathing is used, all the connections must be tight. A receptacle analyzer *(page 26)* will tell you right away whether your receptacles are grounded.

**METAL BOXES**
## Other grounding methods

Grounding clip

Armored cable connector

In a system with metal boxes, the pigtail method shown at right is considered by many to be the most secure. However, other methods also work well if installed correctly. For instance, some systems use a grounding clip to clamp the ground wire to the side of the box.

If a house is wired with armored cable or conduit *(page 35)*, often there is no ground wire. The cable connector joins the metal sheathing or conduit to the box to provide the path for ground.

## In boxes

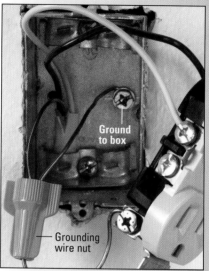

Ground to box

Grounding wire nut

**Metal boxes:** In this secure arrangement, both receptacle and metal box are grounded. Ground wires are spliced together and attached via pigtails to the box and receptacle. A grounding wire nut has been used. It has a hole in its top that makes installing a pigtail easier.

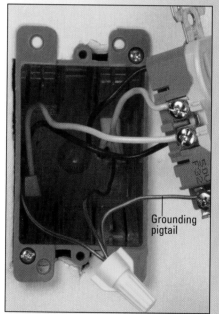

Grounding pigtail

**Plastic boxes:** Where plastic boxes are used, a ground wire typically connects to the receptacle only. Here, where wiring runs through this box to another box, a grounding pigtail is used to connect to the device.

## In fixtures and switches

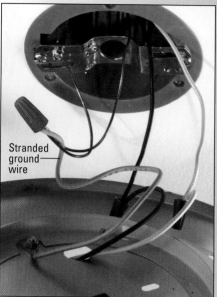

Stranded ground wire

**Old fixtures:** Many older ceiling fixtures are not grounded. Recent codes, however, call for grounding. Connect the fixture's ground lead (usually a stranded wire) to the strap on a metal box or to a ground wire.

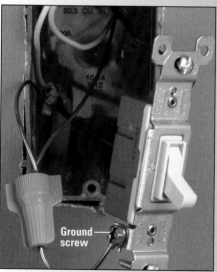

Ground screw

**Old switches:** Like ceiling fixtures, most older switches are not grounded—in fact, many switches do not even have a grounding screw. Recent codes call for switches to be grounded. Replace an older switch with a newer one that has a ground screw and connect to a ground wire.

# DIFFICULT WIRING CONFIGURATIONS

Usually wiring is easy to figure out: A hot wire, a neutral wire, and a ground wire attach to a device or fixture. Sometimes, however, you may find configurations that aren't as clear.

■ **Two cables in a switch box:** Switch wiring may involve two cables entering the box or only one *(page 23)*.

■ **Through wires:** If wires travel through a box but are not connected to a device or fixture, they may belong to another circuit.

■ **Three-way switch:** A switch with three terminals (and three wires connected to it) is a three-way switch *(page 70)*.

■ **Unusual colors:** Some homes have color-coded circuits. For instance, one circuit may have a brown hot wire, while another circuit has a purple hot wire. You will find this only in houses with conduit.

■ **Aluminum wire:** Silver-color wires with "AL" printed on the insulation are aluminum wiring *(page 33)*.

■ **Three-wire cable:** Electricians sometimes save work and materials by using three-wire cable (with a black, red, white, and ground) to carry power from two different circuits. The black wire is attached to one circuit; the red wire to another.

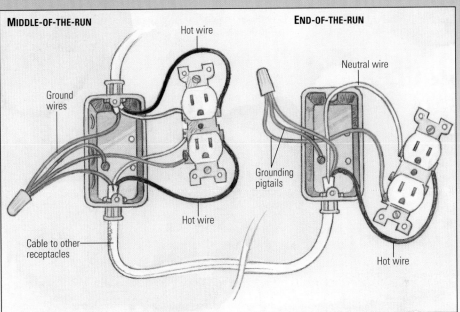

**MIDDLE-OF-THE-RUN** — Hot wire, Ground wires, Hot wire, Cable to other receptacles

**END-OF-THE-RUN** — Neutral wire, Grounding pigtails, Hot wire

If a receptacle is in the **middle of the run,** wires continue through it, delivering power to other receptacles or fixtures. Two cables enter the box. Usually, the two blacks connect to the two brass terminals and the two whites connect to the two silver terminals. Sometimes pigtails are used instead. If only one cable enters a receptacle box, the receptacle is at the **end of the run,** meaning that it is the last receptacle on the circuit. Wiring is simple: black to the brass (gold) terminal and white to the silver terminal.

## WHAT IF...
### Two switches share a box?

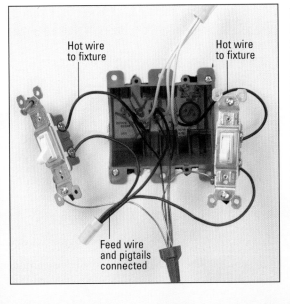

Hot wire to fixture — Hot wire to fixture — Feed wire and pigtails connected

When two switches share a box and are on the same circuit, they may share a single hot wire. The feed wire (the wire bringing power into the box) connects to two pigtails, each of which attaches to a switch. Each switch has another hot wire, leading to its light fixture.

## How a split receptacle works

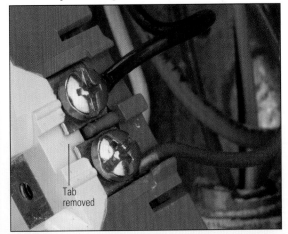

Tab removed

If the tab that joins the two brass terminals has been broken off and two hot wires connect to the brass terminals, the receptacle is "split." Either each outlet is on a separate circuit, or one of the outlets is controlled by a wall switch while the other is always hot.

# MASTERING SKILLS & TECHNIQUES

A clear understanding of how an electrical system works is an important part of basic wiring. Equally important are the techniques that produce safe and secure electrical connections. The skills you need to do your own projects—cutting and stripping wire and making solid connections—are the same ones that professional electricians use every day. You don't need to be as fast as a pro, but your work can and should be as safe and accurate.

## Why good technique matters
If wires are spliced or connected haphazardly, the repair or installation may function—at first. But there is a good chance a wire will work its way loose, creating a dangerous condition.

Wiring the right way is not difficult. It takes only an hour or two to learn how to make splices and connections just as solid as those made by professionals. In fact, using the right technique often proves faster than doing it the wrong way. For example, looping a wire around a terminal screw clockwise *(page 46)* keeps it from sliding away from the screw shaft as you tighten the screw.

## Use the right tools
Before beginning electrical work, gather the basic set of tools described on *pages 10–11*. These tools are designed for wiring; don't scrimp by using general-purpose tools. For example, if you try to strip wires using a knife, you will probably nick the copper and weaken the wire. Twisting wires together using a pair of household pliers is difficult and produces connections that might come apart. With wire strippers and lineman's pliers, making professional-quality connections will be a snap rather than a struggle.

## Safety while working
The most important safety measure is to shut off power and test to make sure power is off *(page 43)*. Review the safety tips on *pages 7–8* before beginning a project.

**Proper splices and connections are the key to safe and durable electrical installations.**

## CHAPTER PREVIEW

**Testing**
*page 42*

**Stripping and splicing wire**
*page 44*

**Joining wire to a terminal**
*page 46*

**Mapping and indexing circuits**
*page 48*

*Lay a small drop cloth (an old towel works well) on the floor or countertop beneath the electrical box you are working on. It will catch all the debris and protect surfaces from scratches. Complete a repair by wrapping all bare wires and wire nuts with electrician's tape for an extra measure of protection.*

Screwdriver

Wire strippers

Long-nose pliers

# TESTING

**E**lectricians keep their testers handy at all times—a practice worth imitating. Make it a habit to test thoroughly for the presence of power before beginning work.

In addition to a receptacle analyzer *(page 26),* a home do-it-yourselfer needs a voltage tester to see if the power is on and a continuity tester to check for broken connections or disconnected wires.

**Good testing habits**

You need no special knowledge to operate a tester. However, work methodically to gain reliable results from your tests:

■ Be sure to make contact with the metal parts you are testing. Pressing hard isn't necessary, but the probe must make direct contact with metal, not plastic insulation or electrician's tape.

■ Insert the voltage tester probes at least an inch into the receptacle being tested.

■ If a wire or screw is painted, use a rubber-grip screwdriver to scrape some paint off before testing it.

## Voltage detector

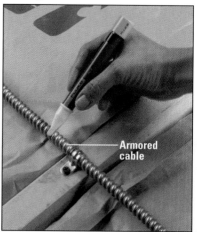

A voltage detector senses power through insulation and metal or plastic boxes. Just hold it on or near a cable, wire, or electrical box and press the detector's button; it will light or buzz to signal the presence of current.

## Test for power

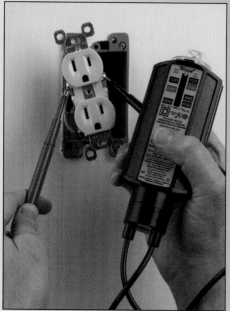

**1** Insert the probes of a voltage tester into the two slots of a receptacle to test for the presence of power. The light will glow or the needle will move if electrical current is present.

**2** Once you have opened a box, test again to be sure there is no current. Hold one probe to each screw terminal on either side of the receptacle, where wires are connected. Also touch each wire.

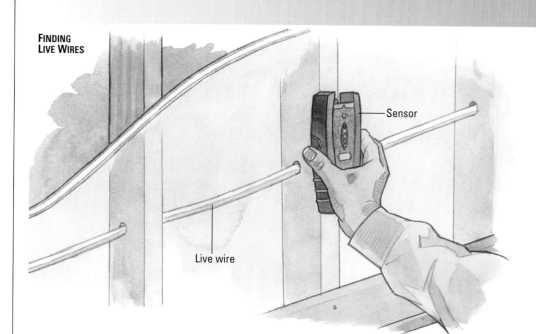

FINDING LIVE WIRES

*Some stud sensors not only detect the presence of joists and studs behind the wall surface, but also indicate the presence of any live wires. Follow the instructions carefully to* *tune the tool to the thickness of the wall. Use a sensor before cutting into a wall or ceiling. It still pays to be safe and probe carefully (page 6) to make sure there are no hidden risks.*

# Test for continuity

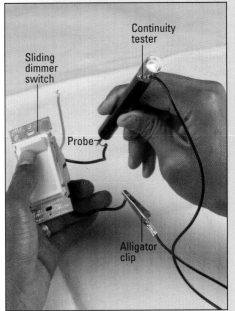

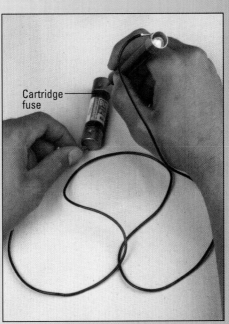

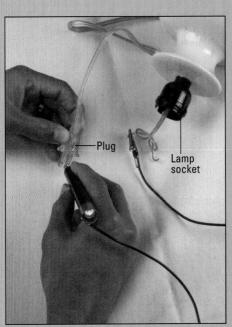

**Switch: Use a continuity tester only when the wiring is disconnected from power.**
To test a switch, attach the alligator clip to one terminal and hold the probe against the other terminal. If the tester glows when the switch is on and does not glow when it is off, the switch is OK.

**Fuse:** To test a cartridge fuse, hold the alligator clip against one end and the probe against the other. If the tester does not glow, the fuse should be replaced.

**Lamp wiring:** To test lamp wiring, attach the tester clip to one end of a wire and touch the probe to the other end. If the tester does not glow, the wire is broken at some point along its length.

---

**STANLEY** PRO TIP

### Test the tester

Testers can malfunction. To make sure it is working properly, always test the tester. Each time you get a reading of no power when using a voltage tester, insert the probes into a receptacle you know is hot. The tester should glow, confirming that it is working properly.

### Avoid cheap testers
You may be tempted to buy an inexpensive tester with a neon bulb. These bulbs are notorious for failing, and they are easily damaged. A reliable tester is well worth a little extra money.

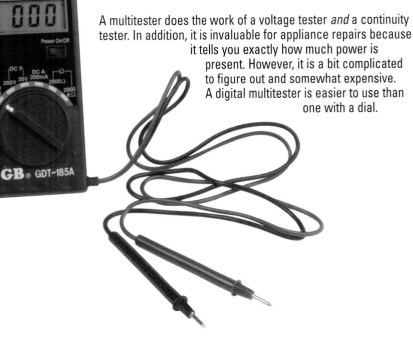

### Consider a digital multitester

A multitester does the work of a voltage tester *and* a continuity tester. In addition, it is invaluable for appliance repairs because it tells you exactly how much power is present. However, it is a bit complicated to figure out and somewhat expensive. A digital multitester is easier to use than one with a dial.

# STRIPPING AND SPLICING WIRE

**B**efore an electrical connection can be made, a wire end must be stripped of its insulation. This is a simple process, but it's important to do it right so the copper wire won't be damaged. Use a good pair of strippers like those shown below.

It will take a bit of practice—say, 15 minutes worth—to learn how to make firm splices. The right tool is essential: Nothing does the job like a pair of lineman's pliers.

Always take a few moments to check your work. Check the bare wire you have just stripped to make sure it is not gouged. After splicing wires and adding the correct size wire nut, tug on the wires to make sure they are securely joined.

*Both of these tools will do a good job stripping wire, but the long-nose strippers get into tight places more easily.*

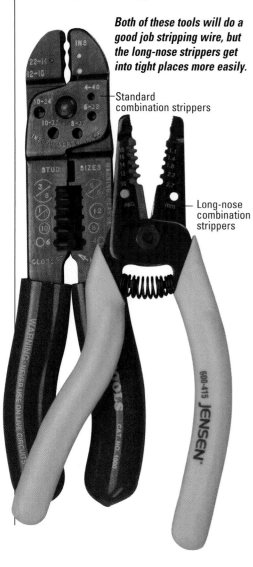

Standard combination strippers

Long-nose combination strippers

## Stripping wire

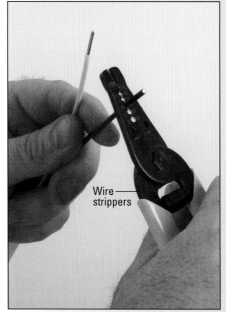

Wire strippers

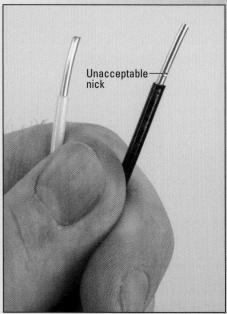

Unacceptable nick

**1** Determine the size of the wire you will strip *(page 35)*. Open the strippers, place the wire in the correct hole, and squeeze them shut. Give a slight twist, then slide the insulation off.

**2** The insulation should slide off easily with no more than a slight mark on the wire. If you have to pull hard or the stripper leaves a nick, check that you are using the right hole. If the problem persists, buy a new pair of strippers.

## Working with cord

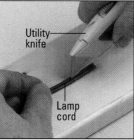

Utility knife

Lamp cord

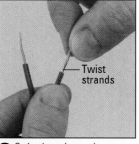

Twist strands

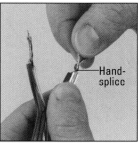

Hand-splice

**1** Separate lamp cord (also known as zip cord) before stripping. Poke the tip of a utility knife between the two wires. Pull the cord to split it.

**2** Strip the wire ends. With your fingers, twist the exposed strands clockwise until tight.

**3** Do not attempt to splice cord wire using lineman's pliers; it's too easy to break strands. Instead, twist the wires together clockwise by hand and add a wire nut.

### How much insulation should be stripped?

If you will be joining the wire to a terminal, remove about ¾ inch. If you will be splicing a wire to another wire, remove about 1 inch.

# Splicing wire

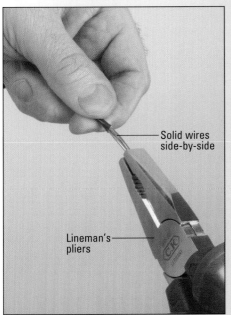

Solid wires side-by-side

Lineman's pliers

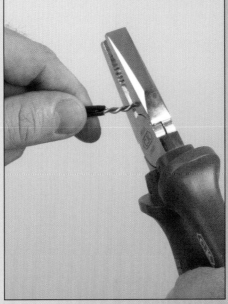

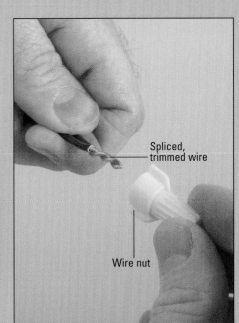

Spliced, trimmed wire

Wire nut

**1** Hold the stripped wire ends tightly next to each other. Grip both with lineman's pliers. Twist clockwise until you feel a slightly stronger resistance, then stop. If you twist too hard, you could break a wire. Practice on some scrap wire before you start a project.

**2** Using diagonal cutters or lineman's pliers, cut the tails off the tip of the splice. This makes it easy to push the splice into a wire nut and assures that both wires will be held firmly together. Trim so that about ¾ inch of spliced wire remains.

**3** Choose a wire nut to fit the size and number of wires you have spliced *(page 13)*. Push the spliced wires in, then twist the nut clockwise to tighten. Tug on the wires to make sure the connection is tight, then wrap the bottom of the nut with electrician's tape.

## WHAT IF...
### Solid wire joins to stranded wire?

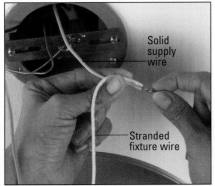

Solid supply wire

Stranded fixture wire

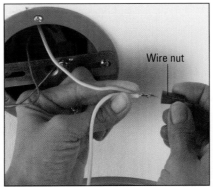

Wire nut

**1** Light fixtures typically have stranded wires that connect to solid feed wires. Strip 1¼ inches of insulation from the stranded wire. Using your fingers, twist the stranded wire tightly around the stripped solid wire, leaving about ⅛ inch of stranded wire sticking beyond the end of the solid wire.

**2** Carefully poke the wires into a wire nut so that the protruding tip of the stranded wire goes as far as possible into the nut. Twist the nut until tight. Tug on the stranded wire to check the connection. Wrap the bottom of the nut with electrician's tape.

**STANLEY**® PRO TIP

### Twist three or more wires all at once

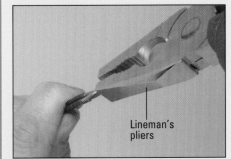

Lineman's pliers

When splicing more than two wires, it's tempting to splice two and then twist the third to the splice. Don't—the wires might break. Instead, grab all three (or four) wires at the same time with your lineman's pliers and twist. It may take you a few attempts to master this technique.

# JOINING WIRE TO A TERMINAL

Joining a wire to a terminal screw seems like a simple procedure. But it's worth a few minutes of time and a little practice to learn how to make a secure connection. Terminal connections come under a lot of stress when devices such as switches or receptacles are pushed into boxes, and one poor connection can create a nasty short.

Wrap the wire almost all the way around the screw before tightening it. Make sure the wire is wrapped clockwise around the terminal screw so that as the screw tightens the loop is pulled in, not out.

In an ideal connection, all the wire under the screw head is stripped and no more. (*Page 36* shows how stripping too much insulation leads to an unsafe situation.)

Most homeowners use long-nose pliers to bend a loop in the wire (see steps at right), but if you plan to install a number of devices, consider purchasing a wire-bending screwdriver.

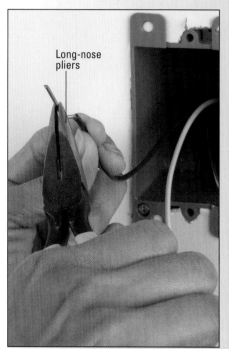

**1** With the tip of a pair of long-nose pliers, grab the bare wire just past the insulation. Twist to the left. Slide the pliers up a little, and bend to the right.

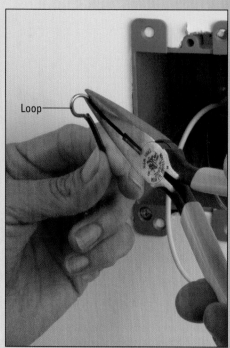

**2** Move the pliers again and bend again to the right. This should complete a partial circle with an opening just wide enough to fit over the threads of a terminal screw.

## WIRE-BENDING SCREWDRIVER
### A perfect loop every time

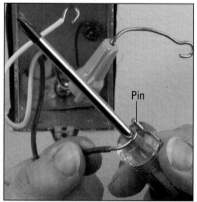

This handy tool makes it easy to form perfect loops in wire ends. Just slip the wire between the screwdriver shaft and the pin and twist.

## SAFETY FIRST
### Avoid push-in connections

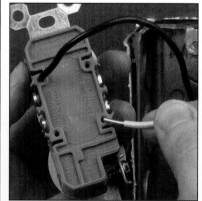

In the back of a switch or receptacle, you'll find connection holes designed to accept stripped wire ends. Using them saves a little time, but the resulting connection is not as secure as one made to a terminal screw.

**STANLEY** PRO TIP

### Save time by bending with long-nose strippers

Some strippers are shaped so their tips act much like long-nose pliers. This allows you to strip and bend without changing tools. You can also use them to squeeze the wire around the terminal (*Step 3*).

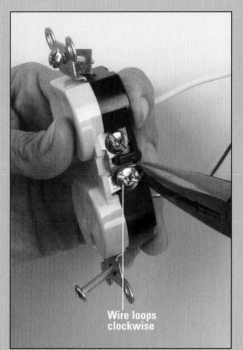

Wire loops clockwise

**3** Unscrew the terminal screw until it becomes hard to turn. Slip the looped wire end over the screw threads. Grab the wire on either side of the screw with long-nose pliers and tighten around the screw.

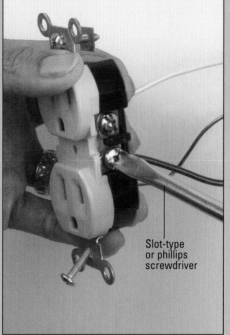

Slot-type or phillips screwdriver

**4** Check that the loop is on the terminal screw clockwise. Tug to make sure the wire cannot come loose. Tighten the terminal screw until the wire is snug between the screw head and the terminal surface.

**5** After all the wires are connected, wrap electrician's tape tightly all around the device to cover the terminal screws.

## WHAT IF...
### The job calls for an unusual connection?

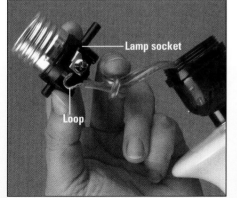

Lamp socket

Loop

**Stranded wire:** To join a stranded wire to a terminal, strip the wire end and twist the strands together *(page 44)*. Use your fingers to form a loop. Wrap the bare wire clockwise around the terminal screw. You may need to push the wire into place as you tighten the screw to make sure no strands slip out.

Pigtail

**Two wires, one terminal:** Never attach two wires to a single terminal. Instead, make a pigtail. Cut a piece of wire about 6 inches long and strip both ends. Splice one end to the two wires you need to connect and attach the other end to the terminal.

Setscrew

**Setscrew terminals:** In service panels, 240-volt receptacles, and other high-voltage connections, you will find setscrew terminals. Loosen the setscrew, poke the stripped wire end into the terminal hole, and tighten the setscrew.

# MAPPING AND INDEXING CIRCUITS

Somewhere inside the service panel—usually stuck on the door—there should be an index that shows which areas of the house are covered by each circuit breaker or fuse. The index will help you shut off power to the correct circuit before working on it.

Codes require service panels to be indexed, but sometimes installers don't bother to trace down each circuit. If there is no index, make one. To complete the index, work systematically to identify the circuit for every electrical outlet in the house. Be prepared to find some odd combinations. In older homes, a single circuit may travel through several floors. Or you may find an entire circuit serving only a couple of receptacles. Avoid attaching family members' names to the index; they might change rooms. Use more permanent directional designations like "east bedroom" or "front hall."

Indexing is easiest working with a helper who can turn circuits on and off while you test the lights, receptacles, and appliances.

## WORKING WITH A HELPER
### Communication methods

If two people are working, the one stationed at the service panel must let the other know which circuit is off. Once the roamer has finished testing outlets, he or she needs to tell the other person to flip the breaker back on and a new one off.

If the house is small, just shouting back and forth can work. In a larger home, use cell phones or walkie-talkies.

If you are working alone, follow this process: Go into every room and flip on all the light switches and lamps. Then, shut off all the circuits except one and look for the lights that are on. To tell from a distance whether a receptacle is on or off, plug in a radio and turn it up loud. Once you know the general area covered by a circuit, test all the receptacles systematically.

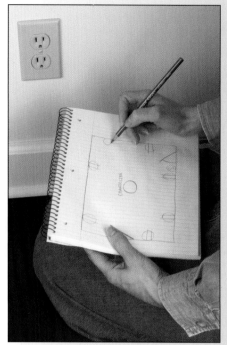

**1** Make a rough sketch of each room in the house, showing the location of all electrical outlets—lights, receptacles, and hard-wired appliances. Don't forget the basement, hallways, attic, garage, and outdoor electrical service.

**2** Flip on all the lights in the house. Assign a circuit number to each fuse or breaker in the service panel. Shut off one breaker or unscrew one fuse.

### USING A CIRCUIT FINDER

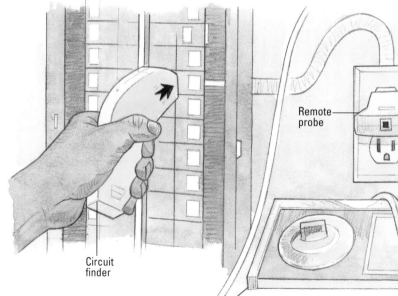

Circuit finder

Remote probe

*A circuit finder enables you to quickly locate which circuit a receptacle is on. Plug the remote probe into the receptacle.*

*At the service panel, point the finder at the breakers until the light glows, identifying the circuit.*

**3** Test outlets throughout the house. Note lights that have turned off. Open the refrigerator door so you can see whether the interior light is on, turn on appliances, and test each outlet in each receptacle.

**4** When you encounter an outlet that has been turned off, mark the circuit number on that room's sketch. After you have tested all outlets, restore power to the circuit you just tested and shut off the next circuit. Work systematically.

**5** Transfer your findings in chart form to a piece of paper that fits the panel door. For clarity, position the circuit numbers near the actual fuses or breakers.

## Situations to watch out for

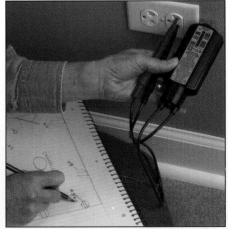

**Same receptacle, different circuits:** The two outlets of a receptacle may be connected to different circuits *(page 39)*. Always check both outlets and mark the drawing accordingly.

**Low-voltage circuits:** Don't forget low-voltage power devices, such as a doorbell. The thermostat is especially important. Crank it all the way up or down so that the heat or air conditioning stays on during the test.

**Appliances:** Test all appliances, such as the garbage disposal, by turning them on. If you have an electric range, air conditioner, or water heater, it should be controlled by a separate 240-volt circuit.

# REPAIRING LIGHTS & CORDS

It may not be worth your while to repair an inexpensive lamp or a small appliance. But if the piece is valuable—for economic or sentimental reasons— you can give it new life with just a little work. The basic tools and techniques presented in the preceeding chapters will equip you to make most of the repairs needed around a home.

### Finding and solving problems

Any electrical repair project begins with safety. **Before dismantling a lamp or appliance, unplug it. Shut off power to the circuit before working on a light fixture.**

To diagnose a problem, you'll often use a continuity tester *(page 43)*. It tells you if there is a break (i.e., a lack of continuity) along the length of a wire, or if the contacts of an electrical device have broken. It can help you isolate and identify the problem: a bad plug, cord, socket, or switch.

Lamps, which plug in, and light fixtures, which are permanently connected to household circuits, are wired in much the same way. Most parts, such as sockets and cords, are widely available and cost little. Repair techniques are largely a matter of common sense: Pull new cord through the lamp to replace the old cord, or replace a faulty socket with a new one of the same type and wire it the same way as the old one.

For best results, work away from distraction. Try to finish a repair in one sitting, so you can remember where all the parts should go.

### Chronic problems

This chapter also demonstrates easy and safe solutions for a circuit that chronically overloads. It shows how to repair damaged wire inside an electrical box. In addition, you'll learn how to replace a dryer cord that does not match up with its receptacle.

## Most problems can be traced with a continuity tester and solved using simple wiring techniques.

### CHAPTER PREVIEW

**Changing lightbulbs**
*page 52*

**When a circuit overloads**
*page 53*

**Plugs and cord switches**
*page 54*

**Lamp sockets and switches**
*page 56*

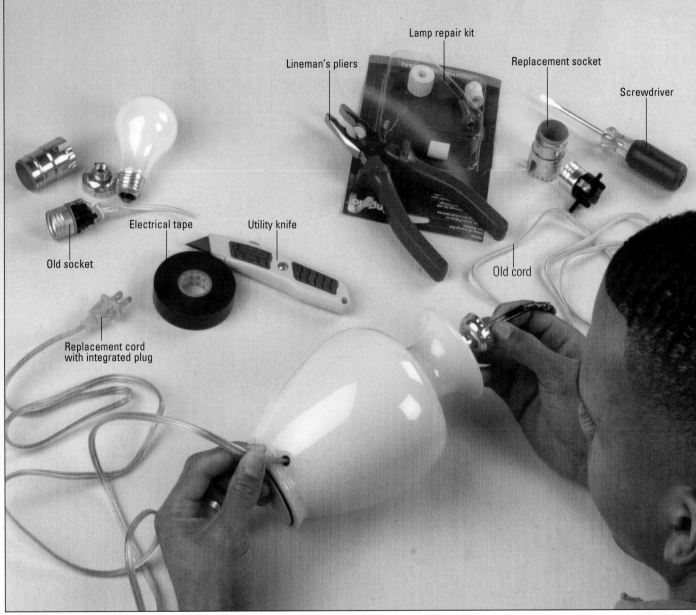

Lamp repair kit

Lineman's pliers

Replacement socket

Screwdriver

Old socket

Electrical tape

Utility knife

Old cord

Replacement cord
with integrated plug

*It's not difficult to completely replace the electrical innards of a lamp. When you finish, the lamp will be as good as new.*

**Rewiring a lamp**
*page 58*

**Fluorescents**
*page 60*

**Chandelier repairs**
*page 62*

**New dryer cord**
*page 64*

**Repairing wiring in a box**
*page 65*

# CHANGING LIGHTBULBS

It takes only one homeowner to change a lightbulb, but you may want to consult with family members before choosing which bulb to use. For instance, if you have to change the bulb in a fixture more than once every few months, buying a long-life bulb will save you both hassle and money. If a light fixture or lamp is brighter than needed, install bulbs of lower wattage or replace the switch with a dimmer *(page 71)*.

If a light stops glowing altogether, chances are you simply need to replace the bulb. If a bulb won't glow unless you screw it in hard, or if the bulb flickers, the problem may be the socket or wiring, not the bulb; see *pages 56–59* for the remedy.

### Get the wattage right
Don't ignore the warning sticker that tells how much wattage a fixture can handle. Installing a bulb of too-high wattage overheats the fixture, causing bulbs to burn out quickly, damaging the fixture and the ceiling material, and creating a potential fire hazard. If you need more light than the fixture can deliver, replace the fixture.

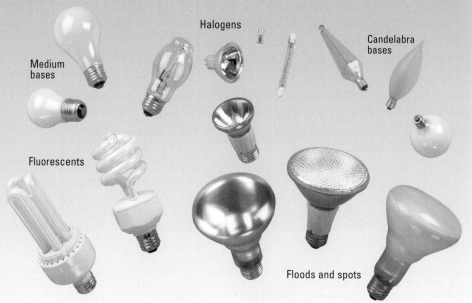

*Make sure the bulb will fit the fixture's socket; several sizes exist. To improve energy efficiency in standard incandescent fixtures, buy a screw-in fluorescent; several shapes and sizes are available. Halogen fixtures deliver more light for the power; see* page 59. *For recessed canister lights, use a flood bulb for general illumination, and a reflector bulb (also called a directional flood) for a spotlight effect.*

*Low-voltage halogen fixtures (pages 100–103) and lamps call for single- or double-ended bulbs. For information on fluorescent tubes, see* page 60.

---

### SAFETY FIRST
**Handling halogens**

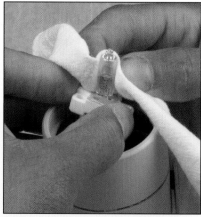

Halogen bulbs get very hot, and they're sensitive to oils—just touching one with fingers can greatly shorten a bulb's life. So let a bulb cool, then handle it with a clean cloth or light gloves.

---

**STANLEY** PRO TIP: **When the bulb breaks**

Changing a lightbulb is no joking matter if the glass has broken. **Make sure the power is off.** Rather than handling it with fingers, gently push a raw potato onto the shards and twist.

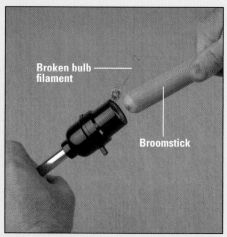

Broken bulb filament

Broomstick

If most of the glass is gone from a broken bulb, insert a broomstick into the bulb's socket and twist it out.

# WHEN A CIRCUIT OVERLOADS

**M**any homes have a similar problem: When you run the toaster and the microwave at the same time, or use a blow dryer while the bathroom fan is on, a circuit overloads, causing a fuse to blow or a breaker to trip.

One solution is to install a new circuit with new receptacles—a messy, expensive job. But there is a simpler solution: Plug that toaster or blow dryer into a receptacle powered by another circuit.

If you have a detailed index of your circuits *(pages 48–49)*, it will be easy to find alternative receptacles. If none is nearby, use an extension cord option, shown below, or hire a pro to install a new circuit.

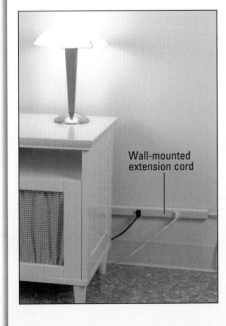

**1** List the items on the problem circuit. Using your circuit index, find out which items can be moved to another circuit to relieve overloading. In this example, moving any of the three items will work. Make sure the change won't overload the other circuit.

**2** Make sure you have the correct size breaker or fuse for the circuit. A circuit using #12 wire can be on a 20-amp circuit; a circuit using #14 wire must be on a 15-amp circuit *(pages 30–31).*

Channel

**3** Plug an extension cord into a receptacle powered by a different circuit (one that is not already overloaded). If none is nearby, consider running an extension cord through a wall-mounted channel.

---

### How much can a circuit handle?

The higher the amperage of a circuit, the more power it can handle. To figure out how many watts a circuit can take, multiply volts by amps. A circuit's safe capacity is only 80 percent of its total capacity. So a 120-volt, 15-amp circuit has a total capacity of 15 amps or 1800 watts (120 × 15 = 1800). A safe capacity for that circuit is 12 amps or 1440 watts.

## Extension cord options

Wall-mounted extension cord

Various solutions are available to extend a circuit's reach without running new cable through walls. One option is a wall-mounted extension cord, which has one or two outlets per running foot. Raceway wiring is another option *(pages 78–79)*, but it involves a little more work to install. Both are somewhat unsightly, though often they can be hidden behind furnishings.

### WHAT IF...
### A fuse blows?

If the metal strip is broken or melted but the window is clear, the fuse has blown because the circuit has overloaded—too much power was used at once *(pages 16–17, 30–31)*. If the window is blackened, a short circuit is the culprit. Check the circuit's wiring for loose or damaged wiring *(pages 36–37)*.

Overload

Short

# PLUGS AND CORD SWITCHES

If a lamp cord and plug are brittle or damaged, rewire the lamp with a new cord that has an integrated plug *(page 51)*. If the plug has a cracked body or loose prongs but the cord is in good shape, install one of the replacement plugs *shown here.*

### Cord maintenance

Always grasp the plug when you pull a plug out of a receptacle. If you tug on the cord, you may loosen or break wiring connections in the plug. Organize and position your cords to minimize tripping hazards.

## PRESTART CHECKLIST

☐ **TIME**
About 10 minutes

☐ **TOOLS**
Phillips screwdriver, cutting pliers, long-nose pliers

☐ **SKILLS**
Cutting and twisting stranded wire, attaching stranded wire to terminals

☐ **PREP**
A clean, well-lighted work surface

☐ **MATERIALS**
Replacement plug, cord switch

## Flat lamp plugs

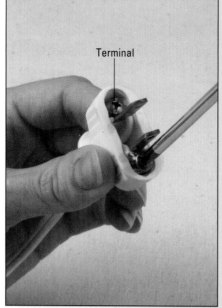

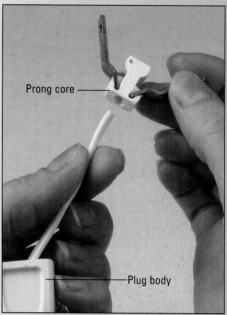

**Screw terminals:** To replace a plug, snip the cord near the old plug, divide the cord, and strip ¾ inch of insulation from the end of each wire. Slip the wires through the replacement plug and connect them to the terminals. Tug to check the connections and make sure there are no loose strands.

**Snap together plug:** To add a squeeze-type replacement plug, snip off the old plug and feed the cord through the plug body. Place the prongs over the cord and push the cord completely into the prong core. Squeeze the prongs tight. Slide the body up and snap it onto the core.

**STANLEY** PRO TIP

### Neutral and hot wires

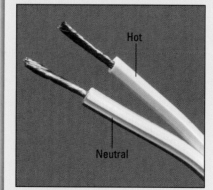

If the neutral and hot wires on a cord get mixed up, a tool or light may be energized when the switch is off. The smooth wire on a cord is hot; connect it to the brass terminal. The wire with ridges (or ribs) is neutral; connect it to the silver terminal.

## Replacement plug options

Flat

90° angle

Industrial

Heavy-duty

*Most replacement plugs connect in much the same manner as the plugs shown at left. The 90° plug allows you to position the cord in several different angles, making it easier to plug into tight spots.*

# Appliance plugs

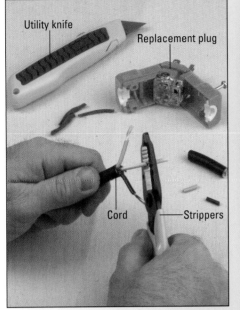

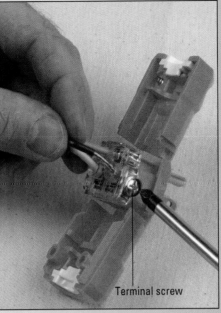

**1** For an appliance, choose a hefty plug with a grounding prong. Working carefully with a knife to avoid cutting into wire insulation, strip about 2 inches of sheathing from the end of the cord. Strip about ¾ inch from the ends of each wire and twist the wire strands tight *(page 44)*.

**2** Slide the replacement plug's body onto the cord. Connect the wires to each of the terminals—black to hot (the narrower prong), green to ground (the round prong), and white to neutral (the wide prong).

**3** Tug on the wires to see that the connections are firm and make sure there are no loose strands. Assemble the plug body and tighten the screws.

## Rotary cord switches

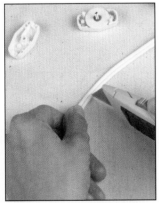

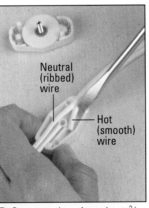

**1** If a lamp switch is hard to reach, install a cord switch. To install a rotating (rotary) cord switch, first cut through the hot (smooth) wire, taking care not to nip the neutral (ribbed) wire.

**2** Separate the wires about ¾ inch on each side of the cut. Push the wires into the body of the switch *as shown*, then screw the two parts of the body together.

## Rocker cord switches

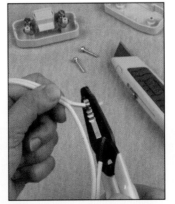

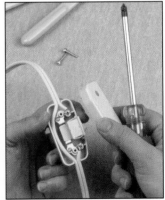

**1** To install a rocker cord switch, snip the hot (smooth) cord without damaging the neutral (ribbed) cord. Separate the wires about 1 inch on each side of the cut. Strip about ¾ inch from the ends of each cut wire and twist the strands tight *(page 44)*.

**2** Push the neutral wire into the switch's groove. Connect the stripped ends to the switch's terminals *(page 47)*. Snap the top part of the switch over the wires and tighten the screws.

# LAMP SOCKETS AND SWITCHES

If a lamp doesn't come on even after you've changed the bulb or if it flickers, check the cord (especially near the plug) for breakage. If you see no damage, unplug the lamp and examine the socket. Often, the problem is not the socket itself but the wire connections to it *(Step 3)*.

The socket *shown on these pages* is the most common kind. Other types are made of plastic or porcelain and attach to the lamp or light fixture via screws or a nut and bolt. Take the old socket to a hardware store or home center for a replacement that fits.

## PRESTART CHECKLIST

☐ **TIME**
About 20 minutes (not including shopping) to test and replace a socket

☐ **TOOLS**
Screwdriver, voltage tester, perhaps strippers and lineman's pliers

☐ **SKILLS**
Fastening wire to a terminal, testing for voltage

☐ **PREP**
A clean, well-lighted work surface

☐ **MATERIALS**
Replacement socket, switch

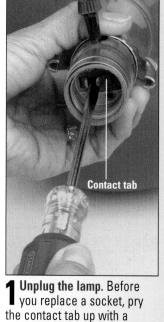

**Contact tab**

Terminal connection

Cardboard sleeve

**1** **Unplug the lamp.** Before you replace a socket, pry the contact tab up with a screwdriver so that it makes stronger contact with the bulb's base. If a contact tab is rusty, scrape it with a slot screwdriver. Plug in again and test the lamp.

**2** If the problem is not solved, **unplug the lamp** and remove the socket. Unscrew the small screw near the contact tab. Squeeze the socket shell and pull it out. (If the shell reads PRESS, put your thumb there when you squeeze.)

**3** If there is a cardboard sleeve, slide it off. Pull up gently on the socket and examine the terminal connections. If you cannot fix the problem by tightening a terminal screw, loosen the screws, remove the wires, remove and test the socket.

## TEST THE SOCKET
### Check for faulty connections

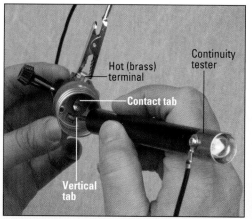

Hot (brass) terminal

Continuity tester

**Contact tab**

**Vertical tab**

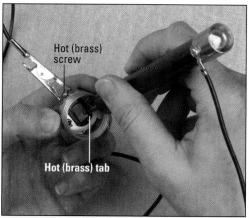

Hot (brass) screw

Hot (brass) tab

If the socket has a switch, attach the clip to the hot (brass) terminal and touch the probe to the vertical tab or the contact tab. The tester should glow with the switch on and not glow with the switch off. If you get other results, replace the socket.

If the socket does not have a switch, attach the clip to the hot (brass) screw and touch the probe to the brass tab, as shown. Then clip onto the neutral (silver) screw and touch the probe to the threads. If the tester does not glow in either test, replace the socket.

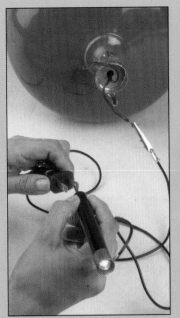

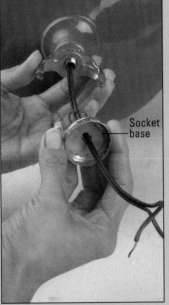

Socket base

Socket base

Underwriters knot

Socket base

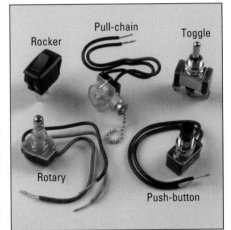

**4** If the socket tests OK, or if you replace the socket and that does not solve the problem, test the wires for continuity. If there is a break in continuity, rewire the lamp *(pages 58–59)*.

**5** If the wire is knotted, untie it. If the socket base has a setscrew, loosen it. Unscrew and remove the socket base. Purchase a new socket that matches the old one.

**6** Screw the new socket base into the lamp. Tighten the setscrew. Tie the cord in an Underwriters knot. Twist the wire strands tight with your fingers and connect them to the terminals *(page 47)*.

**7** Slide on the cardboard sleeve (if there is one) and the socket shell. Push down to snap the shell onto the base.

---

WHAT IF…
## A switch needs replacing on a lamp or ceiling fan?

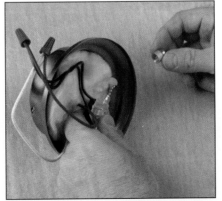

The little switches that attach to the body of a lamp or fixture are notoriously short-lived, but they are also easy to replace. To get at a fixture switch on a lamp, you may have to remove a metal or cloth cover on the bottom of the lamp base. Unscrew the nut, detach the wires, and replace the switch.

A pull-chain switch on a ceiling light or fan mounts in the same way as a lamp switch. To get at one, **shut off power to the circuit,** and remove the fixture's canopy *(page 33)*.

### Fixture switch options

Rocker    Pull-chain    Toggle

Rotary    Push-button

You can usually replace one type of fixture switch with another—say, a toggle with a rocker or rotary switch. The hole in the lamp base is typically a standard size that accepts any of these.

# REWIRING A LAMP

If the socket and the plug are ruled out as the cause of a lamp malfunction, then wiring must be the culprit. No matter what shape or size the lamp, the wiring is essentially the same: A cord runs from the plug to the socket. A multisocket lamp contains a sort of junction box, where the main cord is spliced to shorter cords that lead to individual sockets.

It is rarely a good idea to replace only part of a cord: The splice will be both unsightly and liable to unravel. It's usually not much more work to replace the entire cord.

To divide, strip, and fasten cord wires to terminals, see *pages 44 and 47.*

## PRESTART CHECKLIST

☐ **TIME**
About an hour to rewire a simple lamp

☐ **TOOLS**
Continuity tester, lineman's pliers, strippers, and a screwdriver

☐ **SKILLS**
Stripping wires and connecting them to terminals

☐ **MATERIALS**
Lamp cord with molded plug, or rewire kit containing a cord, and electrician's tape

## Table or floor lamp

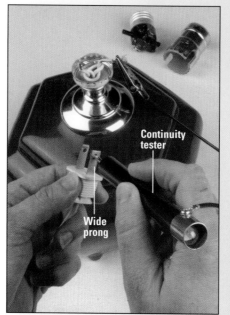

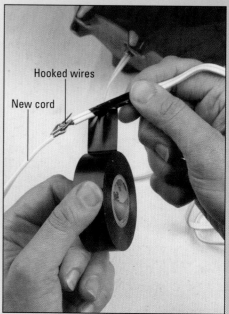

Hooked wires

New cord

Continuity tester

Wide prong

**1** Test wires for breaks in continuity. Attach a tester clip to the wide prong of the plug and touch the probe to the stripped neutral (ribbed) wire at the other end. Repeat for the narrow prong and the hot (smooth) wire. If the tester does not glow for both, replace the cord.

**2** To replace the defective cord, begin by cutting the old cord. Strip about an inch off the ends of the old and new cord wires. Form hooks on all four wire ends and splice the old to the new in a splice that is thin enough to slide through the lamp. Wrap tightly and smoothly with electrician's tape.

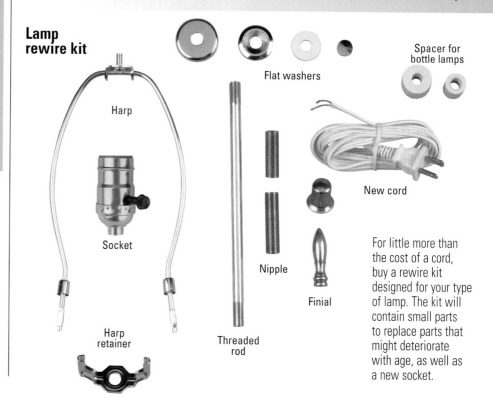

**Lamp rewire kit**

Flat washers

Spacer for bottle lamps

Harp

Socket

Threaded rod

Nipple

New cord

Finial

Harp retainer

For little more than the cost of a cord, buy a rewire kit designed for your type of lamp. The kit will contain small parts to replace parts that might deteriorate with age, as well as a new socket.

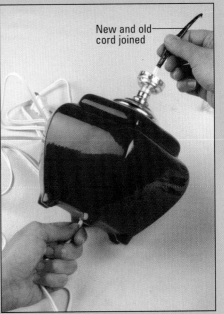

**3** Feed the new cord into the base of the lamp while pulling the old cord through the top. Keep pulling until the new cord emerges. If rewiring a floor lamp, have a helper feed the cord into the base. Separate the cords; discard the old one.

# Desk lamp

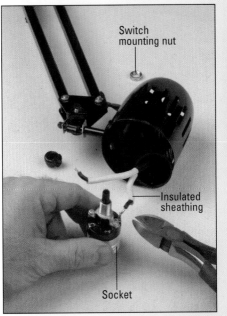

Switch mounting nut

Insulated sheathing

Socket

**1** Unplug the lamp. To remove the socket from a desk lamp, you may need to remove the nut from the twist switch or unscrew a mounting screw located near the contact tab *(page 56)*. Pull the socket out and disconnect the wires from the terminals.

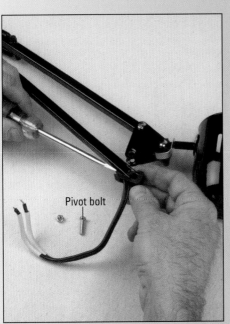

Pivot bolt

**2** Splice the new cord to the old and pull it through, as in Step 2 and Step 3 at left. Pulling may be complicated if the lamp has pivot points; it may require removing a nut and bolt to feed the wire through.

WHAT IF...
**A lamp has two sockets?**

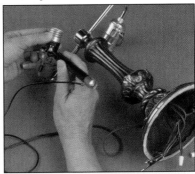

If one socket on a multisocket lamp fails, test the socket. If that is not the problem, open the junction box cover and pull out the tangle of wires. Test the wires leading from the socket to the junction box for continuity *(Step 1 on page 58)*. If all the sockets fail to light, test the cord leading from the plug to the junction box.

**STANLEY** PRO TIP: **Halogen lamps**

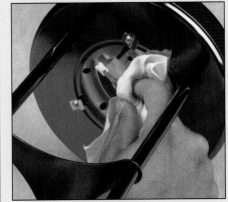

A halogen bulb gets very hot and may burn out if the lamp gets bumped while it is lit. Remove a bulb carefully, using a cloth, and find an exact replacement. If that does not solve the problem, test the socket.

Test the socket with a multitester *(page 43)*. If the reading is lower or higher than the lamp's rating, check the fuse in the lamp for proper amperage. Then test the wires for continuity. If these tests do not reveal a problem, the transformer is probably bad; replace the lamp.

# FLUORESCENTS

**A**new fluorescent fixture is inexpensive and easy to install *(pages 86–87)*, so replacing rather than repairing is often the better option. Before you do, however, quickly check the components in this order: the tube, the starter (if any), the sockets, and the ballast.

Very old fluorescents have both a heavy ballast and a starter. More-recent models have rapid-start ballasts and no starter. The latest models have electronic ballasts, which are nearly maintenance-free.

Fluorescent fixtures are often flimsy. Check that sockets are firmly seated and are not cracked. Tubes should fit snugly between the sockets.

An old delayed-start fluorescent flickers a few times before coming on as the starter delivers a burst of energy to get the tube going. A newer rapid-start fixture has a ballast that supplies extra power when turned on, so the light comes on immediately. A circuline fluorescent differs from rectangular models only in its shape.

## Troubleshooting fluorescents

When faced with the following problems, work your way through the solutions one by one until the light works.

### Does not light
Twist a tube to tighten it or replace the tube. If there is a starter, replace it. Replace a damaged socket. Replace the ballast or the fixture.

### Tube is blackened
If only one end is black, turn the tube around. Replace the tube if both ends are black.

### Flickers or takes a long time to light
Tighten, turn around, or replace a tube. If there is a starter, replace it. Replace the ballast or the fixture.

### Hums and/or seeps black gunk
**Don't touch the seepage with your fingers.** Wear gloves. Tighten the screw securing the ballast. Replace a leaking ballast or the fixture.

## Tubes

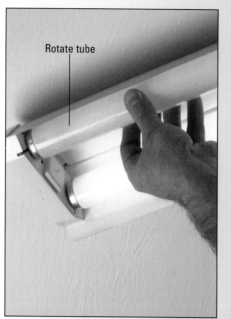

**1** If a tube is black at both ends, replace it *(Step 2)*. If it flickers or does not come on, try rotating it in the socket until it seats firmly or until the light comes on.

**2** To remove a tube, hold both ends and rotate until you feel it come loose at one end. Guide the pins out of the socket. To install a new tube, insert pins into one socket and guide the pins into the other socket. Rotate the tube a quarter turn, until you feel it seat or until it lights.

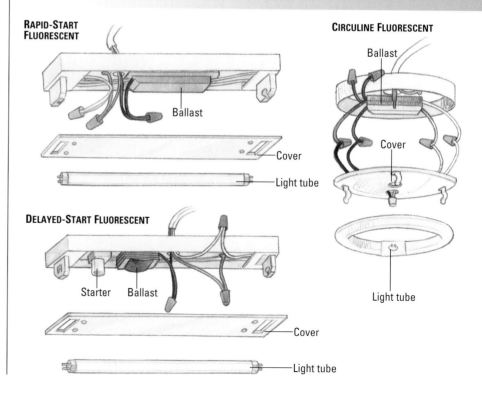

**RAPID-START FLUORESCENT** — Ballast — Cover — Light tube

**DELAYED-START FLUORESCENT** — Starter — Ballast — Cover — Light tube

**CIRCULINE FLUORESCENT** — Ballast — Cover — Light tube

## Starters

If a fixture has a starter, replace it every time you replace a tube. Be sure to buy a starter with the same serial numbers as the old one. If a tube is slow lighting up, tighten the starter. If that does not solve the problem, replace the starter. If the light still doesn't work, the ballast is to blame.

## Sockets

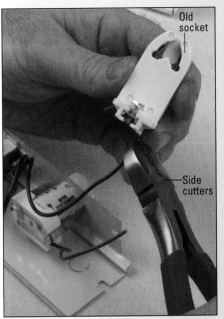

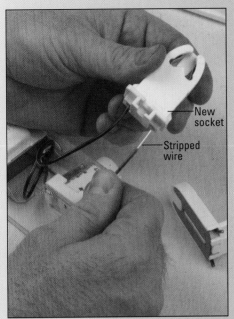

**1** Replace a socket if it is cracked or does not grab the tube firmly. Some sockets just slide out, while others are held in place by a screw. If you cannot remove the wires, cut them near the socket.

**2** Buy a replacement to match the old socket. Strip ¾ inch of insulation from each wire end and push the wire end into the hole of the new socket. Push the new socket firmly to the fixture.

## BALLAST
### Install an exact replacement

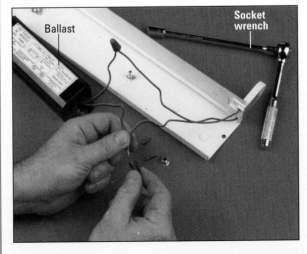

If all the other fixes fail, the ballast is the problem (see the troubleshooting box on *page 60)*. A replacement ballast may cost about the same as a new fixture, but may be a bit less work to install. **Shut off power to the light.** Tag the wires for future reference. Disconnect wires if possible, or cut them. Remove the ballast and install an exact replacement, wiring it just as the old ballast was wired.

**STANLEY** PRO TIP

### Guard tubes from damage

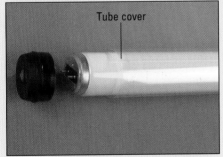

Fluorescent tubes are easily broken and are sensitive to cold. If your fixture lacks a cover and the tubes might get bumped, protect them with a clear plastic sleeve. Covers also help if the fixture has trouble starting in the cold.

# CHANDELIER REPAIRS

**O**lder chandeliers often need repair. Many were manufactured with little regard to the heat that the bulbs produce. Years of overheating have made the wire insulation brittle. A typical fixture has cord running through five or more tubes, allowing several opportunities for malfunctions.

Because they are near a hot bulb and surrounded by glass, sockets and the wires attached to them often deteriorate. If all the lights do not work, the stem wire probably needs to be replaced *(Step 4)*. If some of the wiring needs replacement, consider rewiring the entire fixture—it won't take much longer.

If only one light fails to come on, try pulling up the contact tab inside the socket *(page 56)*. Vacuum dust from the socket. If the bulb still does not light, pull out the socket and test it *(Step 2)*.

## PRESTART CHECKLIST

☐ **TIME**
About 3 hours to dismantle, test, and run new wires in a chandelier

☐ **TOOLS**
Voltage tester, continuity tester, phillips screwdriver, wire strippers, long-nose pliers

☐ **SKILLS**
Testing for power and continuity, stripping and connecting wires

☐ **PREP**
Line up a helper to assist with removing the fixture. Lay a drop cloth on a work surface to cushion the fixture as you work on it.

☐ **MATERIALS**
Cord wire, electrician's tape

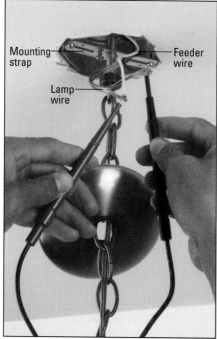

Mounting strap · Feeder wire · Lamp wire

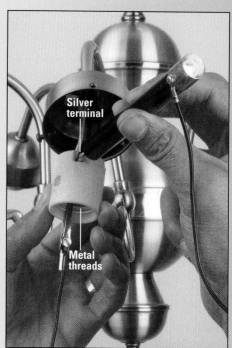

Silver terminal · Metal threads

**1** **Shut off power to the circuit** (in addition to flipping off the light switch). Support the chandelier so it won't fall down. Loosen the screws or screw collar holding the canopy in place and slide it down. Pull the wires apart and test for power *(page 42)*.

**2** Attach a continuity tester clip to the metal threads inside the socket and touch the neutral (silver) terminal with the probe. Then, clip onto the brass screw and touch the probe to the contact tab inside the socket. If the tester light does not come on for both tests, replace the socket *(page 57)*.

**TYPICAL CHANDELIER**

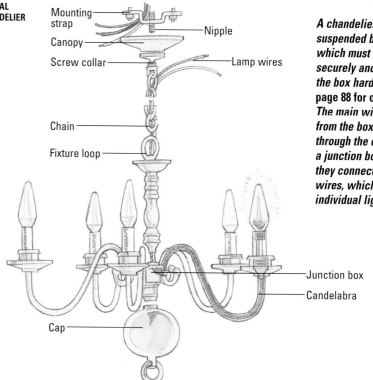

Mounting strap · Nipple · Canopy · Screw collar · Lamp wires · Chain · Fixture loop · Junction box · Candelabra · Cap

*A chandelier is suspended by a chain, which must be securely anchored to the box hardware (see page 88 for options). The main wires run from the box down through the chain to a junction box. There they connect to socket wires, which lead to individual light sockets.*

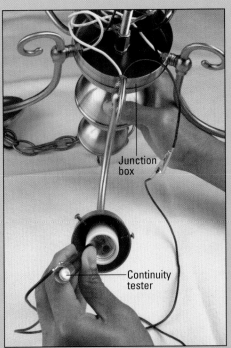

Junction
box

Continuity
tester

**3** Disconnect the wires in the box, remove the chandelier, and place it on a work surface. Open the chandelier's junction box and pull out the wires. Test both the neutral (ribbed) and hot (smooth) wires for continuity.

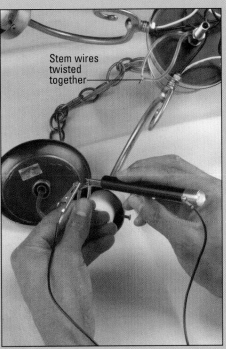

Stem wires
twisted
together

**4** To test the stem wires, twist them together at the junction box. At the other end, attach a continuity tester clip to one wire and touch the probe to the other wire. If the tester does not glow, replace the stem wires.

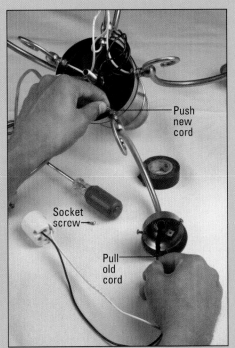

Push
new
cord

Socket
screw

Pull
old
cord

**5** To replace a cord, separate, strip, and splice the old cord to the new. Pull the old wire through until the new wire appears *(pages 58–59)*.

---

**STANLEY** PRO TIP: **Accessing and pulling chandelier wires**

Junction
box

A chandelier's junction box is located in the center of the fixture. To open it, remove the nut at the bottom. Inside you will find a tight mass of wires. Space may be at a premium here, so after rewiring, cut the wires as short as you can. Use the smallest wire nuts possible.

Some chandelier junction boxes are crammed tight with wires. To figure out where a socket wire ends up in the junction box, tug the wires at the socket end and feel the wires at the other end.

Chandelier tubes may be narrow. Join the new cord (using lamp cord, which can withstand heat) to the old with a tight splice *(page 58)*; a bulky splice may stick. If you're still having trouble pulling wires through an old fixture, there may be corrosion in the tubes. Try blowing through the tubes, and run a single wire through the tube to ream out any obstructions.

# NEW DRYER CORD

Older 240-volt electric dryer receptacles have three prongs, attaching to three wires—two hots and one neutral. New codes require a four-prong receptacle, which connects to two hots, a neutral, and a ground wire.

If a dryer cord does not plug into your receptacle, hire a pro to change the receptacle, or change the cord yourself. The following steps show how to change from a three-wire to a four-wire cord. (Do not change from a four-wire to a three-wire. You will be eliminating a ground wire, which offers extra protection against shock.)

## PRESTART CHECKLIST

☐ **TIME**
About an hour to remove the old cord and install a new one

☐ **TOOLS**
Screwdriver, drill, and perhaps strippers

☐ **SKILLS**
Drilling a hole in metal, attaching wires to terminals

☐ **MATERIALS**
A new dryer cord and a grounding screw with a head large enough to capture the cord's ground wire

**1** Purchase a cord with a plug that fits the receptacle. See that the cord amperage rating matches the receptacle.

Old cord
New cord

**2** Remove the access panel at the back of the dryer. Loosen the screws to the strain-relief bracket and remove the old wires. Connect the black, red, and white wires from the new cord to the same terminals.

Strain-relief bracket

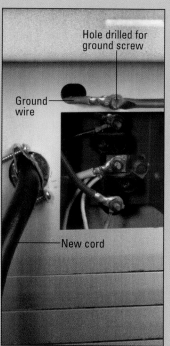

Hole drilled for ground screw
Ground wire
New cord

**3** On the dryer's metal housing, drill a hole slightly smaller than the diameter of the screw shank. Feed the grounding screw through the ground-wire connector and finish tightening the screw.

---

**SAFETY FIRST**
**240 volts pack a wallop**

A shock from 120-volt wiring is painful but probably will not harm an adult. However, 240 volts are more dangerous. Even inserting a plug requires caution. To be safe, **shut off power to the circuit,** plug into the receptacle, and then turn the power back on.

---

**STANLEY** PRO TIP

## Testing a 240-volt receptacle

Voltage tester

If a 240-volt receptacle delivers no power or only partial power to an appliance, check the service panel to make sure power is on. Then very carefully make a live test: Insert the probes of a voltage tester into two slots at a time. You should get a reading of 120 volts in two positions (with one probe in the ground or neutral slot and one in a hot slot) and a reading of 240 volts in one position (with the probes in each of the hot slots). If you get different results, have a pro install a new receptacle.

# REPAIRING WIRING IN A BOX

If a wire is nicked, wrap electrician's tape tightly around the damaged areas. But if wiring in a box is generally brittle and cracked, purchase heat-shrinkable tubing and cover all the wires.

Wire insulation in a box—especially a ceiling fixture box, which gets very hot—becomes brittle more quickly than wiring encased in cable inside a wall or ceiling. So even if the wires you see are badly worn, the wiring hidden in your walls is probably OK.

## PRESTART CHECKLIST

☐ **TIME**
About half an hour to wrap 4–6 wires in a box

☐ **TOOLS**
Heat gun, utility knife, side cutters, and lineman's pliers

☐ **SKILLS**
Splicing wires

☐ **MATERIALS**
Heat-shrinkable tubing (available at home centers and hardware stores)

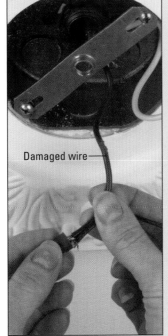

Damaged wire

**1** **Shut off power to the circuit.** Gently pull the wires out and unscrew the wire nuts. If you find thick tape instead of a wire nut, slice it with a knife, taking care not to damage the wire beneath.

Heat-shrinkable tubing

**2** Slide a piece of heat-shrink tubing over the wire, as far as it will go. Cut the tubing to expose the stripped wire end.

Heat gun

**3** Once a wire has been covered with heat-shrinkable tubing, direct a heat gun at the wire until the tubing has at least partially shrunk onto the wiring.

---

**STANLEY** PRO TIP

### Clip and restrip

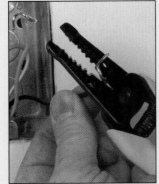

**1** Wire that has been bent twice or more is liable to break. So whenever you install a device or fixture, cut off the previously stripped portion of the wires.

**2** Strip the wire ends *(page 44)*, removing a ¾-inch piece of insulation if you will loop and attach the wire to a terminal, a 1-inch piece if you will splice with a wire nut *(pages 45–47)*.

---

WHAT IF...
### A box is set back?

Codes require that a box be tightly enclosed to prevent an electrical fire from spreading. If a box's front edge is not flush with the wall or ceiling surface around it, slip in a box extender, available in various sizes and made of plastic *(shown)* or metal.

# CONNECTING SWITCHES & RECEPTACLES

It's not unusual for a switch to be flipped on and off tens of thousands of times before it malfunctions—pretty good for a device that may cost less than a dollar. When one wears out, replacing it is a simple job.

This chapter shows how to replace a standard single-pole switch and presents other switches that meet the needs of special situations. These handy devices, such as dimmers and motion-sensor switches, and are just as easy to install as a standard switch.

Receptacles have no moving parts and can last even longer than switches, provided they are not abused. Replacing one is just as easy as putting in a switch.

**Always turn the power off and test a receptacle for power** before you remove the cover plate. Once the box is open, test again for power *(page 42)*. See *pages 32–33* to learn how to safely open boxes to access a switch or receptacle.

Use the tools and skills shown in the previous chapters. To complete these projects, you should be able to strip wire insulation, splice wires, and connect wire ends to terminals.

## Working in a box

Wires inside a box may be short, and space may be tight. Pull out the device and straighten the wires to make working in the box easier. Take your time. A mistake could force you to cut a wire for a second or third time, making it even shorter. If you do need to lengthen a wire, use a pigtail *(page 69)*.

After you have pulled a device out of a box, examine the wiring before you loosen terminal screws. If you do not understand the wiring, you may find it explained on *page 23 or 39*. If the wiring is complicated, tag each wire as you unhook it with a piece of tape that tells you where it should be reattached. Work methodically to ensure a safe and successful installation. Call in a professional if you are still confused.

---

**Replacing and upgrading switches and receptacles call for just a few simple skills.**

### CHAPTER PREVIEW

**Problems with cover plates**
*page 68*

**Replacing single-pole switches**
*page 69*

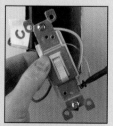
**Replacing three-way switches**
*page 70*

**Installing a dimmer switch**
*page 71*

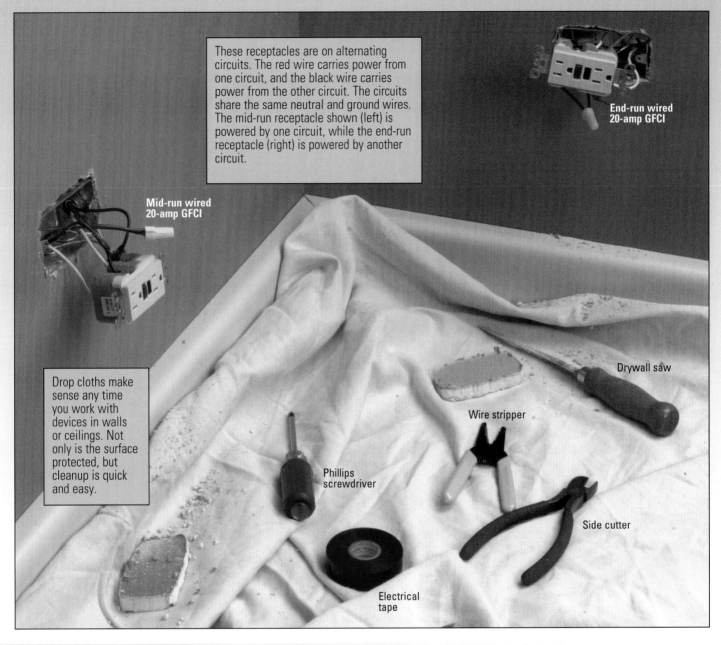

These receptacles are on alternating circuits. The red wire carries power from one circuit, and the black wire carries power from the other circuit. The circuits share the same neutral and ground wires. The mid-run receptacle shown (left) is powered by one circuit, while the end-run receptacle (right) is powered by another circuit.

**End-run wired 20-amp GFCI**

**Mid-run wired 20-amp GFCI**

Drop cloths make sense any time you work with devices in walls or ceilings. Not only is the surface protected, but cleanup is quick and easy.

Drywall saw

Wire stripper

Phillips screwdriver

Side cutter

Electrical tape

**Special-duty switches**
page 72

**Combination switches**
page 74

**Replacing a receptacle**
page 75

**GFCI protection**
page 76

**Surge protection**
page 77

**Raceway wiring**
page 78

# PROBLEMS WITH COVER PLATES

Cover plates are the last line of defense between human hands and live wires. A cracked (or ugly) plate is quickly replaced, and it only takes a few minutes to straighten a device that is out of plumb. (Use a torpedo level if you don't trust your ability to eyeball it.)

Cover plates are available in many styles and can be made of plastic, wood, metal, glass, and ceramic. Cost varies according to style and material, but even a plain, inexpensive plate can be easily dressed up.

One option is paint. With the cover plate installed, use a roller that is slightly damp with paint, so paint does not seep into the receptacle slots.

It is also possible to wrap a cover plate with wallpaper or a small art reproduction.

## PRESTART CHECKLIST

☐ **TIME**
About 10 minutes to adjust or replace a cover plate

☐ **TOOLS**
Screwdriver with a small slot head, drill, level

☐ **PREP**
Lay a towel or small drop cloth on the surface below the device

☐ **MATERIALS**
Have on hand plenty of receptacle and switch cover plates—they're inexpensive

**1** If a cover plate is crooked or doesn't cover the wall completely, note which direction it needs to move. **Shut off power to the circuit** and remove the plate. (A receptacle is shown here, but this will also work with switch plates.)

Phillips screwdriver

**2** Loosen the screws that hold the device to the box. Slide the device until it is plumb, tighten the screws, and place the cover plate on. (If you have a small level, hold it firmly against the device to check its alignment.)

## Oversize plates

If a standard–size cover plate cannot cover damage to a wall, a slightly oversized plate may do the trick.

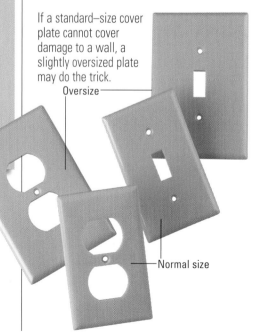

Oversize

Normal size

## WHAT IF...
### A box needs straightening?

Occasionally, a box may be so out of plumb that you cannot straighten the device. To straighten it, **shut off the power** and pull the device off to the side. Drill a hole in the side of the box and drive a drywall screw through the hole and into a nearby stud. Be careful not to nick any wires.

# REPLACING SINGLE-POLE SWITCHES

If a switch fails to turn on a light, or if its toggle feels loose, replace it.

A single-pole switch is the most common type of switch. It has two terminals (not counting the ground), and its toggle is marked with ON and OFF. If three wires attach to it (not counting the ground), it's a three-way switch: *see page 70* for more on those.

Replace a single-pole with an exact match, or install a dimmer or special switch *(pages 71–73)*.

## PRESTART CHECKLIST

☐ **TIME**
About 20 minutes to replace a single-pole switch

☐ **TOOLS**
Screwdriver, strippers, side cutters, long-nose pliers, and a voltage tester

☐ **SKILLS**
Be able to strip wires and fasten them to a terminal

☐ **PREP**
Lay a towel or small drop cloth on the surface below the switch

Voltage tester

**1** **Shut off power to the circuit,** so that the switch cannot turn the light on. Remove the cover plate. Unscrew and pull the switch out gently. Test to make sure there is no power in the box.

**2** Check the wires and terminals. If they look like they've been handled before, cut and restrip. Otherwise, loosen the terminal screws and pull off the wires.

**3** Form loops with wire ends, wrap clockwise around terminals, and tighten screws. Wrap device with electrician's tape to cover terminal screws and any bare wire. Reinstall switch and cover plate.

**REFRESHER COURSE**
## Cut and restrip wire ends

**1** To make sure a wire won't break after being bent several times, cut off the bare end using a stripper or side cutters.

**2** Place the wire in the proper size hole on the stripper, give a slight twist and slide the insulation off. Bend the wire into a loop.

**STANLEY** PRO TIP

### Pigtail short wires

If the feed wires in the box aren't long enough to easily connect a device, don't try to pull more slack into the box—you might damage the wires. Instead, make a pigtail—a 6-inch-long wire stripped at both ends *(page 47)*. Splice one end to the incoming wire and connect the other end to the terminal.

**Assure grounding:** If your system has metal boxes and no ground wire so that sheathing acts as the ground *(page 38)*, remove the little cardboard or plastic washers from screws to make a firm contact between the device and the box.

**Testing**
To test for power, see *pages 42–43.* To attach wires to terminals, see *pages 46–47.*

# REPLACING THREE-WAY SWITCHES

If a switch does not have ON and OFF written on its toggle and has three terminals (not counting the ground), it is a three-way. Two three-way switches can control the same fixture. With a three-way switch, you may turn the light on or off by flipping the toggle either up or down.

If one or both of a pair of three-ways fails to control the light, replace the faulty switch or switches. If the toggle is wobbly, replace the switch.

If you keep track of which wire goes where, replacing a three-way is not much more difficult than replacing a single-pole switch *(page 69)*. If you forget to tag the wires, however, the proper connections can be difficult to figure out.

## PRESTART CHECKLIST

☐ **TIME**
About 25 minutes if you remember to tag the wires; possibly much longer if you forget

☐ **TOOLS**
Screwdriver, side cutters, voltage tester, strippers, and long-nose pliers

☐ **SKILLS**
Stripping wires and joining them to terminals

☐ **PREP**
Lay a towel or small drop cloth on the surface below the switch

☐ **MATERIALS**
One or two three-way switches, wire and wire nuts for pigtails, electrician's tape

**1** **Shut off power**, remove the cover plate, pull out the switch, and **test for power** *(page 42)*. A three-way switch has a common terminal, a different color than the other two traveler terminals. Tag the wire that connects to the common terminal.

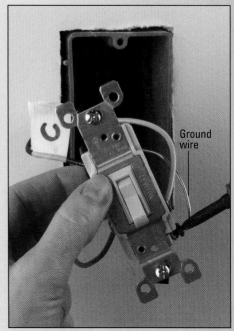

**2** Cut and restrip wire ends *(page 65)* and form them into loops. Connect the ground wire. Connect the tagged wire to the common terminal and the other two wires to the traveler terminals (it doesn't matter which wire goes to which traveler terminal).

---

**STANLEY** PRO TIP

### If you forget to tag wires

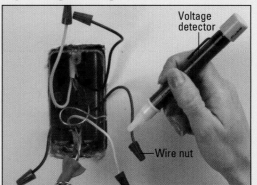

Separate all the wires and place a wire nut on the end of each. Restore power to the circuit. Use a voltage detector to find out which wire is hot. If none is hot, flip the toggle on the other three-way switch and check again. **Shut off power.** Connect the hot wire to the common terminal and the other two wires to the other two terminals.

---

WHAT IF…
**It's a four-way switch?**

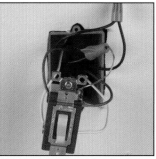

If three switches control the same fixture, two are three-ways and one is a four-way switch. A four-way has four terminals (plus a ground). Before removing the switch, tag each wire. Two wires connect to input terminals; two to output terminals. If the wires aren't tagged, it will take a pro to hook up the switch.

# INSTALLING A DIMMER

In addition to the common rotary dimmer, you can opt for a sliding dimmer like the one shown at right, or a dimmer that looks like a standard toggle switch.

Do not use a standard dimmer switch for a ceiling fan—you'll not only damage the fan, but the switch as well. Instead, install a dimmer made specifically for fans. If two three-way switches control a fixture, you can replace only one of them with a three-way dimmer switch.

Cut and restrip wire ends before splicing them to the new switch *(page 65).*

## PRESTART CHECKLIST

☐ **TIME**
About 20 minutes to replace a single-pole switch with a dimmer switch

☐ **TOOLS**
Screwdriver, side cutters, voltage tester, lineman's pliers, and strippers

☐ **SKILLS**
Stripping and splicing stranded wire to solid wire

☐ **PREP**
Lay a towel or small drop cloth on the surface below the switch

☐ **MATERIALS**
Dimmer switch, wire for pigtails, wire nuts (they may come with the switch), electrician's tape

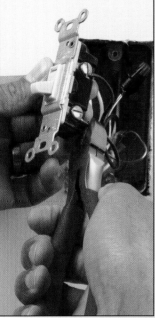

**1** **Shut off power to the circuit.** Remove the cover plate, pull the switch out, and **test to make sure there is no power** *(page 42).* Loosen the terminal screws and remove the wires. Cut and restrip the wires.

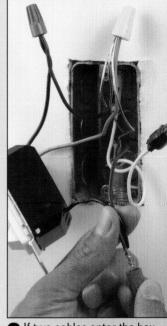

**2** If two cables enter the box, connect the grounds. Splice the white wires together. Splice each black lead to each black wire. One cable entering the box indicates it is at the end of the circuit.

**3** Fold the wires back as you push the dimmer into the box. It is bulkier than a regular switch, so the box may be a little crowded.

### WHAT IF ...
**A three-way dimmer is needed**

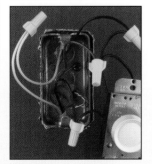

You can use a three-way dimmer for one of the switches—the other must be a toggle. Wire a dimmer as you would a regular switch, except splice wires rather than connecting to terminals.

### ONE CABLE
**End-line wiring**

If only one cable enters the box, splice one lead to the black wire and one lead to the white wire (which should be marked with black).

### **STANLEY** PRO TIP

**Enough wattage?**

An inexpensive dimmer switch that is rated for 600 watts can handle most ceiling fixtures. However, if that switch will control a large chandelier, add up the watts of all the bulbs; you may need a switch with a higher rating.

# SPECIAL-DUTY SWITCHES

The simplest way to improve a home's lighting is to install a switch that does more than turn the lights on and off. This project is usually no more complicated than installing a standard switch.

Examine a switch carefully before buying it. Some special-duty switches are available as three-ways *(page 70)* and can be installed only if you have two cables entering the switch box *(see Pro Tip on opposite page).*

Installing a special switch is similar to installing a dimmer *(page 71).* **Shut off power to the circuit before removing switch.** Connect the switch's ground wire to the house ground. To be sure that wires will not break after being rebent, cut and restrip all wire ends before you connect them to the new switch *(page 65).*

## PRESTART CHECKLIST

☐ **TIME**
About 25 minutes to remove an existing switch and install a special switch

☐ **TOOLS**
Screwdriver, side cutters, and strippers

☐ **SKILLS**
Stripping wire and splicing stranded to solid wire

☐ **PREP**
Lay a towel or small drop cloth on the surface below the switch

☐ **MATERIALS**
Special-duty switch, wire nuts (they may come with the switch), and electrician's tape

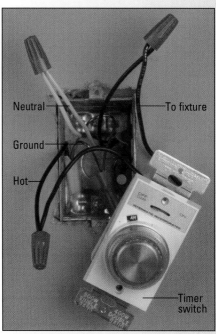

Neutral — Ground — Hot — To fixture — Timer switch

**Timer switch:** A timer switch turns lights on and off once a day. Most commonly, it is used for outdoor lights. Connect the grounds and splice the neutral (white) wires to the white lead. Splice each black lead to a black wire.

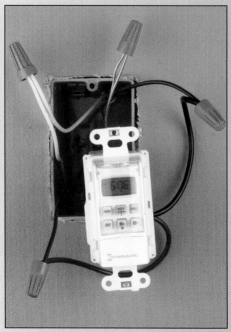

**Programmable switch:** Use a programmable switch to turn lights on and off more than once a day. It can fool a potential robber into thinking people are at home while they are away on vacation. Wire this switch just as you would a dimmer switch *(page 71).*

## Remote-control switch

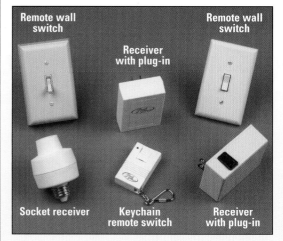

Remote wall switch · Receiver with plug-in · Remote wall switch · Socket receiver · Keychain remote switch · Receiver with plug-in

If you have a fixture controlled by a pull-chain switch and would rather use a wall switch, consider installing one of these devices. They operate by remote control, so you don't have to run cable through walls. To install one, open the fixture and wire the receiving unit, following manufacturer's instructions. Put a battery in the sending unit, which contains the switch. Mount it anywhere on the wall.

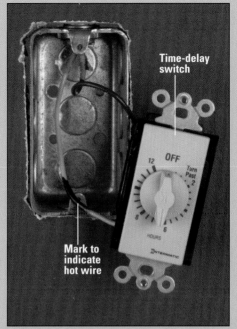

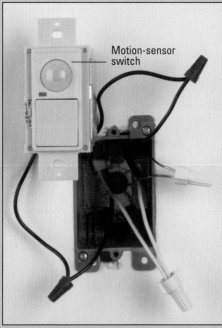

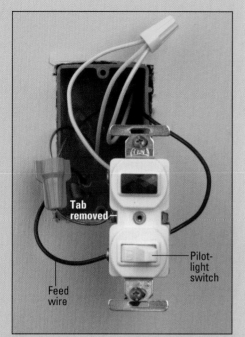

**Time-delay switch:** With a time-delay switch, crank the dial to turn the fixture on and set it to turn off after a specified time. This is useful for fixtures that are risky or expensive to run—a bathroom vent fan or a space heater, for instance. Wire it as you would a dimmer switch *(page 71)*.

**Motion-sensor switch:** A motion-sensor switch turns its light on when it senses movement in the area, then turns the light off after a specified time. (Some models allow you to determine how long the light stays on.) Wire it as you would a dimmer switch *(page 71)*.

**Pilot-light switch:** A pilot-light switch has a small bulb that glows when the device, such as a fan, is turned on. Connect the white wires to the silver terminal (you may need a pigtail) and connect the grounds. Attach the feed wire to the brass terminal without a connecting tab and connect the other black wire to the other brass terminal.

**STANLEY** PRO TIP

### Some switches need two cables in the box

There are two ways to wire a switch *(page 39):* Through-wiring brings power into the switch box and then out to the fixture. End-line wiring brings power to the fixture; a single cable runs from the fixture to the switch box, and the white wire should be marked black. If a switch has more than two leads, it can be installed only if two cables enter the box.

### Other switches

Plug-in timer

Hour electronic time switch

Touch-control dimmer

Browse the electrical department of a home center to find even more special-duty switches. A plug-in timer (left) turns a floor or table lamp on and off at set times. A 20-amp hour timer switch (center) lets you run an attic fan or pool filter motor for 2, 4, 8, or 12 hours. A touch-sensitive dimmer (right) turns the light up, down, on, or off with the tap of a finger.

# COMBINATION SWITCHES

These devices combine two functions. Correctly installed, they are just as safe as two individual switches.

Combination switches are always installed with through-switch wiring and never with end-line wiring. That means you will find two or three cables entering the box *(page 39)*.

Before removing a malfunctioning special switch, tag the wires—and the old switch as well—so you can remember exactly where each wire goes. Purchase a switch to match the old one; ask a salesperson if you are not sure.

**Shut off power to the circuit before removing the old switch.** To be sure that rebent wires will not break, cut and restrip the wire ends before you connect them.

## PRESTART CHECKLIST

☐ **TIME**
About 30 minutes to remove an old combination switch and replace it

☐ **TOOLS**
Screwdriver, side cutters, strippers, long-nose pliers

☐ **SKILLS**
Stripping wire and connecting wire to terminals

☐ **PREP**
Lay a towel or small drop cloth on the surface below the switch

☐ **MATERIALS**
Combination switch, electrician's tape, wire for pigtails

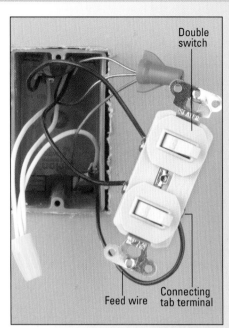

**Double switch:** Squeeze two switches into the space of one. Three cables enter the box: one brings power, the other two run to separate fixtures. Connect the grounds and splice all the neutral (white) wires together. Attach the feed wire to a terminal with the connecting tab. Connect the other two black wires to terminals on the side with no tab.

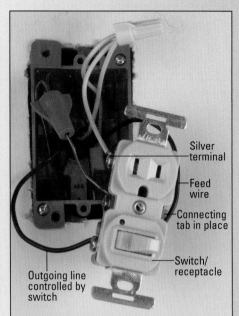

**Unswitched plug:** To make the plug always hot (not controlled by the switch) on a switch/receptacle, start by connecting the grounds. Attach a white pigtail to the silver terminal and splice all the neutral (white) wires together. Connect the feed wire to a terminal with the connecting tab. Screw the other black wire onto the brass terminal on the side with no connecting tab.

## WHAT IF ...
### A switch controls a receptacle?

To have a middle-of-the-run receptacle controlled by the switch, connect the grounds. Make a white pigtail and connect it to a chrome terminal on the side of the device that doesn't have a connecting tab. Splice all the white wires together. Attach the black feed wire to the brass terminal that is not attached to the connecting tab. Attach the outgoing black to one of the black terminal screws next to the connecting tab.

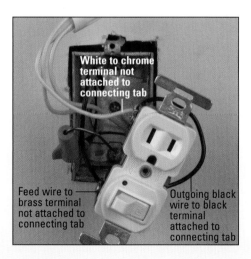

**Feed wire**
This is the wire (usually black or red) that brings power into the box.

**Grounding**
For information on connecting ground wires, *see page 38*.

# REPLACING A RECEPTACLE

A new receptacle is inexpensive and easy to install, so don't hesitate to replace one that is cracked or caked with paint. If a receptacle fails to deliver power, **shut off power to the circuit**, pull the receptacle out, and make sure all the wires are firmly connected to its terminals.

Install a grounded (three-hole) receptacle only if it will be connected to ground *(page 38)*. If the wires connected to it are #14, install a 15-amp receptacle; if the wires are #12, install a 20-amp model.

If wiring is complicated, tag wires with pieces of tape to make clear which wire goes where.

## PRESTART CHECKLIST

☐ **TIME**
About 30 minutes to remove an old receptacle and install a new one

☐ **TOOLS**
Screwdriver, side cutters, strippers, long-nose pliers

☐ **SKILLS**
Stripping wires and joining them to terminals

☐ **PREP**
Lay a towel or small drop cloth on the surface below the receptacle

☐ **MATERIALS**
Receptacle, electrician's tape

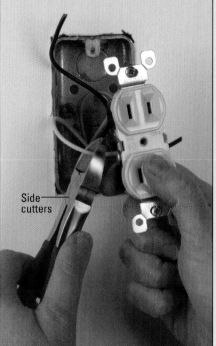

**1** **Shut off power to the circuit.** Remove the cover plate and the mounting screws, and gently pull out the old receptacle *(pages 32–33)*. **Test for power.** Loosen the terminal screws and remove wires, or use side cutters to cut the wires.

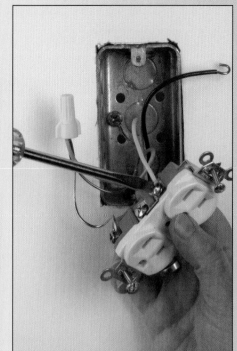

**2** Strip the wire ends, bend them into loops, and connect them to the terminal screws. Connect the hot (black or colored) wires to brass terminals and the neutral (white) wires to silver terminals. Connect the grounds.

## Spec-rated receptacles

Most homeowners turn to the bargain bin for their receptacles. Those work just fine. But if a receptacle often gets bumped, or if people yank on cords when pulling plugs out, consider upgrading to a spec-rated (commercial) receptacle.

**Making connections**
For tips on connecting wires to terminals, see *pages 46–47*.

**WHAT IF...**
## A receptacle is on two circuits?

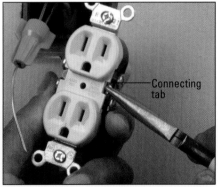

Connecting tab

If more than two wires connect to a receptacle, look at the tab that connects the two hot (brass) terminals. If it is broken off, the receptacle is split, meaning either that it is on two circuits or that one half is switched *(page 39)*. Break off the tab on the replacement receptacle before wiring it.

# GFCI PROTECTION

**I**f electricity goes astray (as in a shock or a short), there will almost always be a change in the flow of current between the hot and neutral wires. A ground fault circuit interrupter (GFCI) shuts itself down immediately upon sensing any such change. Install a GFCI wherever a receptacle might get wet, such as in a bathroom, near a kitchen counter, or outdoors.

Note that GFCIs can malfunction so that they provide power but not safety. To make sure one is still protecting you, check it at least once a month by pushing the "test" button.

## PRESTART CHECKLIST

☐ **TIME**
About 25 minutes to remove a receptacle and install a GFCI

☐ **TOOLS**
Screwdriver, side cutters, strippers

☐ **SKILLS**
Stripping and splicing wire

☐ **PREP**
Lay a towel or small drop cloth on the surface below the receptacle

☐ **MATERIALS**
GFCI receptacle, wire nuts, electrician's tape

Old receptacle

**1** **Shut off power to the circuit.** Remove the cover plate, pull the receptacle out, and **test for power** *(pages 32–33)*. Cut and restrip the wire ends *(page 65)*.

New GFCI

**2** If you wire a GFCI into the middle of a circuit, all the receptacles down the line will also be protected by it. Connect the wires that bring power into the box to the LINE terminals and the wires that go out from the box to other receptacles to the LOAD terminals.

**3** Wrap the device with tape and push it back into the box. Because a GFCI is bulkier than a standard receptacle, take extra care folding the wires into the box behind it.

## WHAT IF...
### Only one receptacle needs protection?

If you want to protect only this receptacle and not others down the line, connect only to the LINE terminals. If the receptacle is in the middle of the run *(page 39)*, add bypassing pigtails *(page 47)* to feed the other receptacles.

**STANLEY** PRO TIP

### Finding LINE and LOAD wires

To protect all the receptacles on a circuit, install a GFCI at the beginning of the circuit run *(pages 16–17)*. If you don't know which wires bring power into the box and which lead to other receptacles, remove the wires, spread them out so they do not touch each other, and cap with wire nuts. Restore power and use a voltage tester to find out which is the hot wire. Connect it and its companion neutral wire to the LINE terminals. Connect the other wires to the LOAD terminals.

# SURGE PROTECTION

**U**tilities provide power that generally is steady and constant. Your lights may flicker occasionally due to a drop in power that lasts less than a second. This is normal and does no damage. Less common, the power coming into your house may suddenly increase, or surge, for an extremely short time. This will not damage most electrical components but may harm a computer, modem, or other electronic equipment.

Telephone lines also may carry unwanted current surges. In fact, modems are damaged by surges more often than items plugged into household receptacles.

A surge arrester senses any increase in voltage and directs it to the ground wire so it can flow harmlessly into the earth. Surge protection works only if your household electrical system is grounded *(page 18)*.

For most homes, all that's needed is a good quality plug-in surge protector (called an arrester or suppressor) or two. For your office, choose a protector that includes a phone connection to safeguard the modem. If you have state-of-the-art audio/visual equipment, plug those components into a surge protector as well.

### Lightning protection

In rural areas, houses can sometimes be damaged by lightning. The devices shown here will not protect your electrical system against a lightning strike. Consult with a local electrical contractor to see if you should install lightning protection.

A bolt of lightning hitting your house can cause a fire. To protect against that, install a lightning rod mounted on the roof, fastened to a wire that runs into the ground. When a bolt of lightning strikes the house, the rod directs much of the power into the earth.

If lightning strikes overhead power lines near your house, the burst of power can fry your service panel or house wires and fixtures. Surge arresters mounted in the service panel are designed to direct excess voltage to the house ground. Consult with contractors and your local building department to see if a device like this could make your home safer.

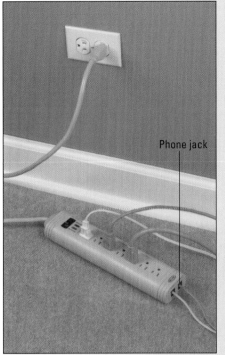

Phone jack

**Simple protection:** A simple power strip like this not only protects against surges, but also makes it easy to organize your cords.

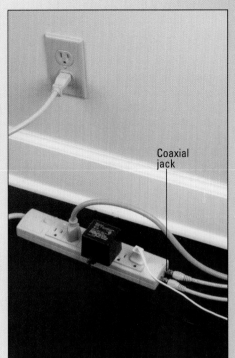

Coaxial jack

**Protect a TV:** This surge protector has a coaxial jack to protect a TV from a surge through the cable.

## Whole-house surge protector

To protect all receptacles and lights from surges, have a whole-house surge protector installed. It is wired directly into the service panel.

Fully protecting an electrical system from a direct lightning strike is not possible. However, this device may keep your wires from harm since lightning damage is not usually caused by direct strikes. It will help protect sensitive electronic equipment from damage due to a power surge traveling through local service lines.

# RACEWAY WIRING

If you need a new receptacle or a new light and switch, the usual procedure is to run cable inside walls. That is a complicated, messy job. In fact, cutting and patching walls takes much more time than the wiring. Wall-mounted raceway wiring eliminates that trouble. The drawback to raceway wiring is the unsightly channel mounted on the wall. If used in a living area, however, raceway can be hidden behind furnishings.

## Planning the job

Choose plastic raceway *(as shown here)* or metal raceway, which can be painted. Have a salesperson help you assemble all the raceway parts you need: a starter box, channel, clips, cover plates, and elbows if you need to turn a corner. You'll also need enough black, white, and green wire for the length of your run. Use #14 wire for a 15-amp circuit and #12 wire for a 20-amp circuit.

## PRESTART CHECKLIST

☐ **TIME**
About 3 hours to install two new receptacles

☐ **TOOLS**
Drill, screwdriver, level, strippers, side cutters, hacksaw, lineman's pliers

☐ **SKILLS**
Stripping, splicing, and connecting wires to a terminal; cutting metal or plastic channel; driving screws into a wall

☐ **PREP**
Spread drop cloths on the floor

☐ **MATERIALS**
Raceway components, plastic anchors, wire nuts, electrician's tape, screws

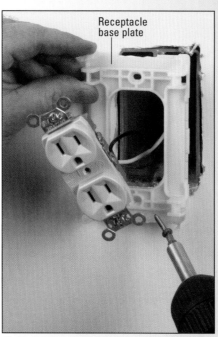

**1** **Shut off power** to the circuit and pull out an existing receptacle *(pages 32–33)*. **Test for power.** Screw the base plate to the electrical box.

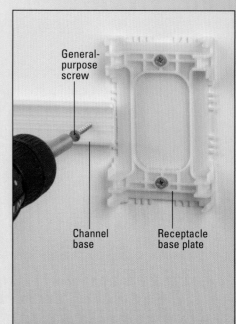

**2** Attach receptacle base plates wherever you want a new receptacle. With a hacksaw, cut pieces of channel to fit between the plates. Screw them to the wall. Where possible, drive screws into studs for solid mounting; otherwise, use plastic anchors to attach screws to wallboard.

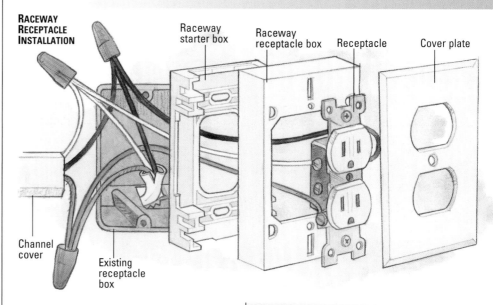

*Raceway components include a starter box, receptacle box, channel, and clips. Use green-insulated wire for the ground.*

**Do your codes allow raceway?**
Check your local building codes to see whether raceway is permitted. You may be required to use metal rather than plastic parts.

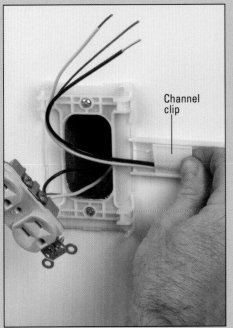

Channel clip

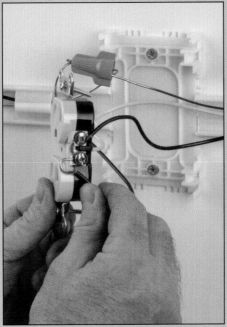

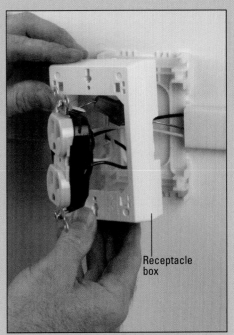

Receptacle box

**3** Insert black, white, and green wire into the channels and secure them with the clips provided. Leave about 8 inches of wire at each receptacle box or starter box.

**4** Connect wires to the new receptacles—black wires to brass terminals, white wires to silver terminals, and green wires to ground.

**5** Connect wires to the old receptacle to supply power. Snap on the covers for the channel. Attach the covers for the new receptacle boxes and install cover plates.

## Metal raceway

Metal components cost a bit more, but they withstand more abuse than plastic, and they can be painted. Install the parts on the wall, then push wires through the channels.

**Stripping and joining**
For tips on stripping and joining wires, see *pages 44–47*.

**SUPPLY POWER**
## Options for connecting to existing wires

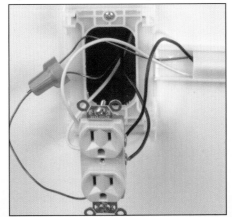

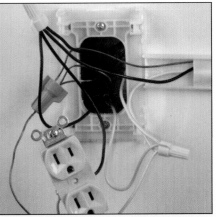

**End of run:** If the existing receptacle is at the end of a run *(page 39)*, connect the raceway wiring to the two open terminals—black to the brass terminal, white to the silver terminal. Pigtail the ground *(page 38)*.

**Middle of run:** If the existing receptacle is in the middle of a run *(page 39)*, remove wires from two of the terminals and connect to terminals with pigtails, as shown.

# INSTALLING LIGHTS & FANS

**N**o matter how old your electrical system, it is always possible—and usually easy—to remove an old wall or ceiling fixture and install a new one. A new fixture can dramatically change the appearance of a room. You can replace a ceiling light with a plain light, a chandelier, track lighting, or even a ceiling fan. See *pages 82–83* for more lighting options.

## Mounting hardware

If your home was built after World War II, attaching a new fixture will be easy. Mounting hardware has changed little, and the new fixture should come with all the parts you need. Simply attach a strap to the ceiling box, and perhaps a center stud as well. Splice the wires, screw the fixture to the strap or the stud, and you are done.

If you have an older home, the old fastening hardware may not line up with the new fixture. Fortunately, home centers carry adapters to solve this problem.

If the new fixture's canopy (the part that snugs up to the ceiling) is smaller than the old one, you may have to paint or patch the ceiling. A medallion *(page 85)* can hide the problem and save work.

Installing a ceiling fan or a heavy chandelier calls for removing the electrical box and installing a heavy-duty "fan-rated" box *(pages 92–93)*.

## Wiring a light or fan

**Shut off power before removing an existing fixture. Test the box for power** after removing the fixture *(pages 6–7)*. To assure a conductive and long-lasting splice, cut and restrip old wire ends *(page 65)* before joining them to the stranded leads *(page 45)* of new fixtures.

Wiring a light or fan is straightforward: Splice white lead to white wire, black to black, and connect the grounds. Installing a new fixture where there was none before is more involved and best left to a professional electrician or someone with experience running new cable. Running cable through walls is a time-consuming and complicated task.

---

## Installing a new light fixture is an easy way to make a dramatic change in any room.

### CHAPTER PREVIEW

**Choosing lights**
*page 82*

**Flush-mounted lights**
*page 84*

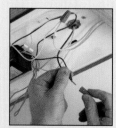

**Fluorescents**
*page 86*

**Pendant lights**
*page 88*

Wall lights are wired just like ceiling lights, only the mounting hardware differs. A center stud or a swivel strap allows the light to be adjusted so it is plumb. Outdoor fixtures have foam or rubber gaskets to seal out moisture.

To avoid straining the wires, cut and bend a coat hanger to support the fixture while you attach the wires.

*Replacing a light fixture is an easy upgrade that usually takes no more than an hour or two. A porch light is no exception. Shut off power. Work on a stable ladder if the fixture is out of reach.*

**Track lights**
*page 89*

**Ceiling fan box**
*page 92*

**Ceiling fan**
*page 94*

**Motion-sensor outdoor light**
*page 97*

# CHOOSING LIGHTS

A light fixture's packaging tells how high in wattage the bulb or bulbs can be. Installing bulbs of higher wattage will damage the fixture, and the bulbs will burn out quickly.

An existing light may seem adequate, but often a room benefits from a brighter light. Buy a new fixture that provides more light than the old one. Install bulbs of lower wattage if it turns out to be too bright.

In living and dining rooms, you may want bright light at some times, and a mellow effect at other times. If so, install a dimmer switch *(page 71)*.

### Canopies to cover
After removing an old fixture, measure its canopy—the part that attaches to the ceiling. If the new fixture has a smaller canopy, you will have to paint and maybe patch the ceiling. Or you may purchase a medallion, a round decorative piece that covers up ceiling imperfections *(page 85)*.

### Pendant lights
The lower a light hangs down, the more attention it commands and the more focused its light becomes. Most pendant lights hang by chains; the lamp cord runs through the links to the fixture. Some modern versions have a decorative cable, and some use a pipe, through which the cord runs. A pendant light may be a chandelier with many arms and bulbs, or it may have a single bulb surrounded by a shade or a globe.

Chandeliers have numerous bulbs, often encased in decorative glass. A chandelier that hangs over a dining room table should be a foot or so narrower than the table and hang about 3 feet above the table. Control a chandelier with a dimmer switch to achieve both brilliant and subdued effects.

If you don't like the look of newer style chandeliers, seek out a dealer who specializes in refurbishing old fixtures. An older chandelier that is completely rewired will be as reliable as a new unit.

A one-piece pendant light is often used in an entryway. Hang it in the center of the room, at least 6½ feet from the floor, so people won't bump their heads.

A pendant light with a shade directs most of its light at a table or counter directly below, although it can also provide general illumination if the shade is translucent. A small fixture can be hung as low as 24 inches above a tabletop. Just make sure the bulb will not shine directly into people's eyes when they are seated at the table.

### Flush-mounted lights
A flush-mounted light fastens against the ceiling or wall. A ceiling-hugging fixture in the middle of a room may be all that is needed to light a bedroom or small dining room. Wall-mounted fixtures are ideal for illuminating bathrooms, especially near a vanity mirror. Sconces work well in hallways.

Most flush-mounted fixtures use standard incandescent bulbs, but energy-saving fluorescents and halogens are available. A "semiflush" fixture hangs down a few inches and casts light upwards at the ceiling, for a more even distribution of light.

If you cannot find a light fixture that is both pleasing and affordable, the best choice

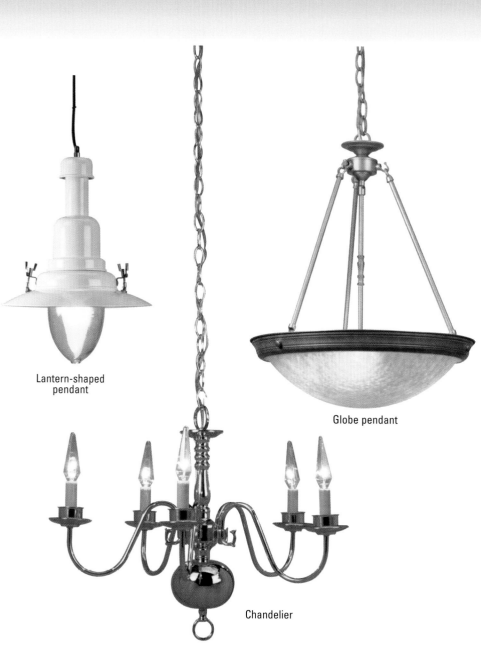

Lantern-shaped pendant

Globe pendant

Chandelier

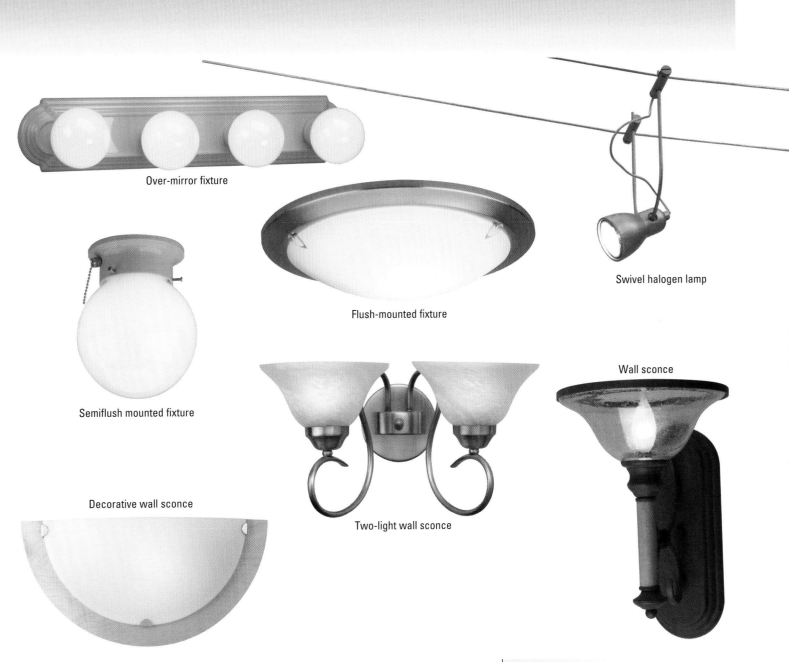

Over-mirror fixture

Swivel halogen lamp

Flush-mounted fixture

Semiflush mounted fixture

Wall sconce

Decorative wall sconce

Two-light wall sconce

may be to buy an inexpensive flush light and paint its canopy to match your ceiling.

Sconces and other wall-mounted fixtures install much like ceiling lights, except they mount on a wall. Such fixtures typically attach to a box, using a strap and nipple *(page 85)* so they can be leveled easily.

If a sconce will be mounted less than 7 feet above the floor, purchase one that doesn't stick out too far from the wall. Some sconces shine upward and provide ambient lighting; others point out or down to illuminate stairs or provide subtle lighting in a hallway.

### Other types
Sleek fixtures that hang from wires or twist in whimsical shapes add a contemporary look. They use low-voltage halogen bulbs, which save energy but get very hot.

In addition to the lights shown here, consider fluorescent *(pages 86–87)* and track lighting *(pages 89–91).* To light the area in or under a cabinet, see *pages 100–101.*

### Recessed canisters need new cable
In some cases a recessed canister light can replace a single fixture. Typically, though, canisters are installed in a series. That means running new cable through walls and ceilings—an advanced procedure best left to the pros or experienced do-it-yourselfers.

# INSTALLING FLUSH-MOUNTED LIGHTS

**R**eplacing a ceiling fixture is a simple job. The hardware that held the old fixture typically can be reused to attach the new. If not, a new fixture most often comes with all hardware needed to install it.

When buying a fixture, make sure it is designed to provide the amount of light you want in a room. Compare its wattage with the old fixture. Don't install bulbs that exceed recommendations, or you will dangerously overheat the fixture and its box. Choose a fixture with a canopy large enough to cover any imperfections in the ceiling, or use a medallion *(page 85)*.

If possible, ground the new fixture. If it is being installed in a metal box, connect the fixture ground lead to the box and to the house ground wire. Check local building codes. Wires in a ceiling box may have cracked or brittle insulation due to overheating. See *page 65* to repair them.

## PRESTART CHECKLIST

☐ **TIME**
About half an hour to remove a fixture and install a replacement, as long as there are no problems with the hardware

☐ **TOOLS**
Screwdriver, strippers, side cutters, voltage tester, and a ladder

☐ **SKILLS**
Stripping wire and splicing stranded wire to solid wire

☐ **PREP**
Spread a drop cloth on the floor below, and set up a stable, nonconductive ladder

☐ **MATERIALS**
Replacement fixture, wire nuts (the ones that come with the fixture may be too small), and electrician's tape

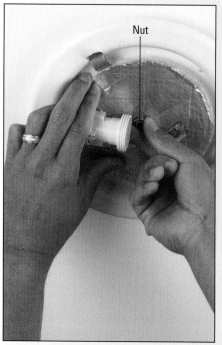

**1** **Shut off power to the circuit.** Open the fixture *(page 33)*. Remove the nut or screws holding the fixture to the box and pull the fixture down. Remove the wire nuts and **check for power in the box** *(page 42)*. Pull the leads off the house wires and remove the fixture.

**2** If the existing mounting hardware will not fit the new fixture, or if it doesn't have a grounding screw, remove it and attach a new strap to the box.

**STANLEY** PRO TIP: **Attaching to older boxes**

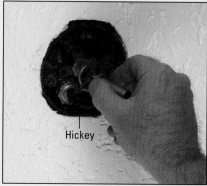

An older "pancake" box like this may have a ⅜-inch pipe running through the middle. To install a center-mount or pendant fixture, use a hickey, which has two sets of threads, one for the pipe attached to the pancake box and the other for a center stud. A hickey is helpful for wiring chandeliers because it has an opening through which a cord can run.

If the pipe protrudes too far, purchase a mounting strap with a hole large enough to accommodate the pipe. Or attach the strap off center by drilling pilot holes in the box and driving sheet-metal screws through the slots in the strap and into the box. However, make sure the fixture's canopy is large enough to cover the box.

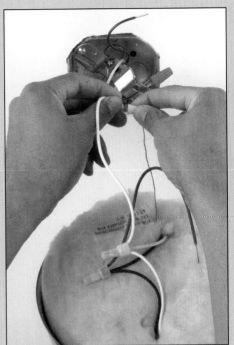

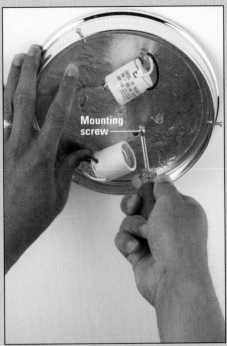

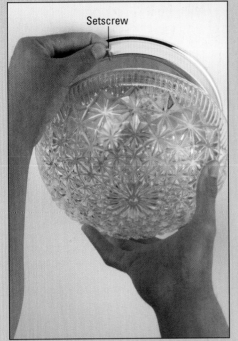

Setscrew

**3** If the fixture is heavy, support it with a coat hanger wire while you work *(page 81).* Connect the ground wire. Splice white lead to white wire and black to black. Wrap the wire nuts with electrician's tape. The insulation may be difficult to work around, but don't remove it; it's a safety feature.

**4** Fold the wires up into the box. Start one mounting screw, then the other, then tighten them. If the fixture has keyhole-shaped screw holes, attach the screws to the box, slip the fixture over the large holes, rotate the canopy so the screws fit into the smaller slots, and tighten the screws.

Mounting screw

**5** The setscrews that hold the globe may already be in the base or may have to be installed. Push the globe to raise the lip above all the setscrews, then hand tighten all the setscrews evenly.

## WHAT IF...
### The new fixture canopy doesn't cover the old hole?

If the new canopy is not large enough to cover up holes or unpainted portions of the ceiling—or simply to add a decorative touch—purchase a medallion. Hold it against the ceiling while you wire the fixture. Before tightening the canopy, see that the medallion is centered.

## MOUNTING SCREWS
### Installing a center-mounted fixture

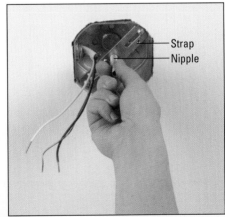

Strap
Nipple

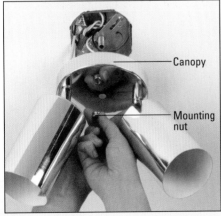

Canopy

Mounting nut

**1** Some fixtures mount with a nipple (short threaded pipe) and a nut in the center, rather than two screws. Install a strap and screw in a nipple. If the nipple that comes with the fixture is too short or too long, purchase another one.

**2** After wiring the fixture, slide the canopy up so the nipple pokes down through the center hole. Screw on and tighten the mounting nut.

# INSTALLING FLUORESCENTS

**F**luorescent lighting is inexpensive to run, but the most common tubes produce light that has a cold, industrial feel. For a little more money, buy tubes labeled "warm" or "full spectrum," which produce light that is much more suitable for a home. Adding a translucent lens diffuses the light and reduces the glare.

It is not difficult to replace an incandescent fixture with a fluorescent one. However, if your goal is simply to save energy costs, a simpler solution is to install a fluorescent bulb in an incandescent fixture *(page 52)*.

An existing fluorescent light might have cable running directly into it, with no electrical junction box. That's okay—the fixture's housing is usually considered adequate for protecting spliced wires.

Because fluorescent fixtures are bulky, enlist a helper when removing an old fixture and installing a new one.

## PRESTART CHECKLIST

☐ **TIME**
About an hour to remove a fixture and install a new fluorescent

☐ **TOOLS**
Screwdriver, drill, strippers, side cutters, voltage tester, lineman's pliers, and a ladder

☐ **SKILLS**
Stripping and splicing wires, driving screws

☐ **PREP**
Spread a drop cloth on the floor beneath the light, and set up a stable ladder

☐ **MATERIALS**
New fluorescent fixture, wire nuts, screws, and electrician's tape

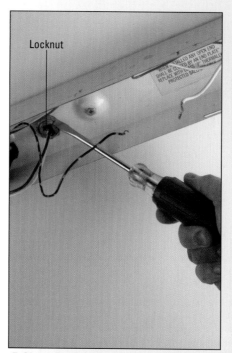

Locknut

**1** **Shut off power to the circuit.** Remove the wire nuts and untwist the house wires from the fixture wires (or snip and restrip them—*page 75*). Loosen and remove the locknut that holds the cable clamp to the fixture.

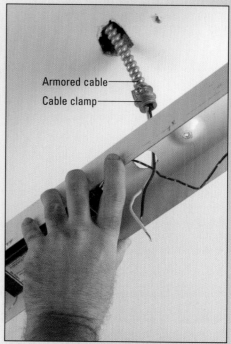

Armored cable
Cable clamp

**2** Remove the screws holding the fixture in place—usually there are several driven into ceiling joists. Support the fixture as it comes loose and guide the wires out through the hole. Note the locations of the ceiling joists. Mark the new fixture to line up screws with joists when you install it.

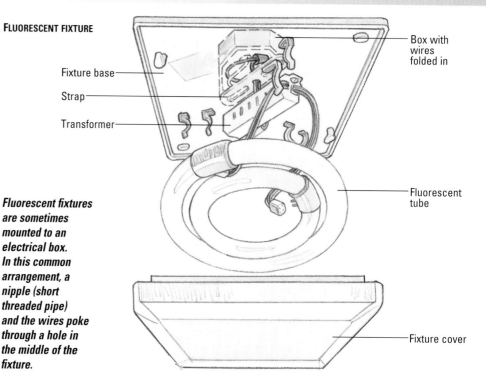

**FLUORESCENT FIXTURE**

Fixture base

Strap

Transformer

Box with wires folded in

Fluorescent tube

Fixture cover

*Fluorescent fixtures are sometimes mounted to an electrical box. In this common arrangement, a nipple (short threaded pipe) and the wires poke through a hole in the middle of the fixture.*

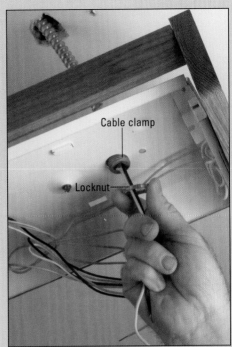

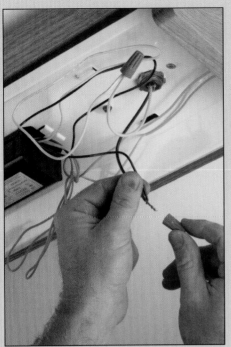

**3** With a hammer and screwdriver, punch open a precut knockout hole in the top of the fixture, then twist off the piece with pliers. Thread the wires through the hole and attach the cable clamp to the fixture with the locknut.

**4** Have a helper hold the fixture up against the ceiling. Drive the screws into joists.

**5** Wire the fixture. Connect the ground wires together and to a grounding screw on the fixture. Splice white fixture wire to white house wire and black to black. Install the fixture tubes and cover.

## Circuline fixture

A round fluorescent fixture is usually mounted to a box. Thread the house wires through the hole in the middle and splice them to the fixture wires. Start driving both mounting screws into the electrical box, then tighten.

WHAT IF…
### The defective fixture is in a suspended ceiling?

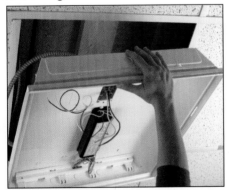

**1** To replace a fluorescent fixture in a suspended ceiling, **shut off power to the circuit.** Remove the ceiling panels around the fixture. Remove the diffuser, disconnect the wires, unscrew the locknut, and pull out the cable (*Steps 1 and 2 above*). With a helper, lift the old fixture out and set the new fixture in place in the ceiling frame.

**2** Clamp the cable and splice the wires, as in *Steps 3 and 5 above*. Replace the ceiling panels, install tubes, and slip on the diffuser.

# INSTALLING PENDANT LIGHTS

**R**eplacing a flush ceiling fixture with a pendant light (chandelier) is usually a simple project. Study the pendant's mounting system before you buy it and make sure you have all the parts you'll need.

To adjust the height of a fixture that hangs by a chain, remove or add links. Use two pairs of pliers to open and close them. On other types, you may need to cut a hanging cable or alter the length of a cord and tighten a locknut.

If the pendant light is heavy, make sure the box is strong enough to hold it; it may require a fan-rated ceiling box *(pages 92–93)*.

## PRESTART CHECKLIST

☐ **TIME**
About two hours to remove an existing fixture and install a new pendant fixture

☐ **TOOLS**
Screwdriver, long-nose pliers, strippers, side cutters, lineman's pliers, voltage tester, and a nonconducting ladder

☐ **SKILLS**
Stripping wire, splicing stranded wire to solid wire

☐ **PREP**
Spread a drop cloth on the floor; set up stable ladder

☐ **MATERIALS**
New pendant fixture, wire nuts, and electrician's tape

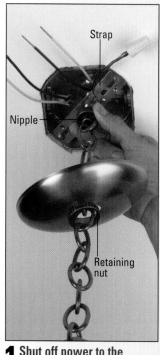

**1** **Shut off power to the circuit** and remove the old fixture *(page 84)*. Screw a nipple into a strap so the nipple hangs down about ¾ inch. Screw on the fixture retaining nut.

**2** Thread wires up through the chain. Cut and strip the wire ends. Splice the ribbed wire to the house's white wire and the other wire to the black house wire. Connect the grounds.

**3** Fold the wires into the box. Slide the canopy up against the ceiling, and tighten the canopy nut.

**STANLEY** PRO TIP

## All on board?

It's easy to get a pendant fixture installed, only to find a part has been left out. Work carefully and install parts in order. On a fixture with a chain, be sure to slide the canopy onto the chain, then thread the wires all the way through the chain and retaining nut before making electrical connections.

**Get the height right**
If people will walk under a pendant light, it should be at least 6½ feet high.

## WHAT IF...
### The fixture has a down rod or retaining ring?

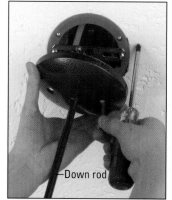

A pendant light with a solid down rod or a round cord typically attaches to the canopy with two hold-down nuts, one on either side of the canopy. The canopy attaches to the box with two screws.

Some lightweight pendant fixtures with chains are not screwed into the box. The chain is secured to the canopy by means of a retaining ring. Nuts attach the canopy to the box.

# INSTALLING TRACK LIGHTS

**T**rack lighting offers plenty of options for style, layout, and design. You can install the track in a straight line, or form a T, L, or H shape *(page 90)*. Choose from among a variety of lamp styles. Place them anywhere on the track and point them in any direction. You can even use two or more types of lights, some for general illumination and others to highlight work areas or spotlight a work of art.

At some point the track must cross over a light fixture box to grab power via a mounting plate. Sketch your planned installation and show the drawing to a salesperson, who can help assemble all the parts needed: track, mounting plate, lamps, and other fittings. Chances are a kit will supply everything needed.

## PRESTART CHECKLIST

☐ **TIME**
About four hours to remove an old fixture and install about 8 feet of track with a turn or two, as well as several lamps

☐ **TOOLS**
Screwdriver, tape measure, strippers, drill, side cutters, voltage tester, lineman's pliers, stud finder, and a nonconducting ladder

☐ **SKILLS**
Measuring accurately, driving screws into joists, stripping wire, and splicing stranded wire to solid wire

☐ **PREP**
Spread a drop cloth on the floor and set up one or two ladders. A helper will come in handy when installing long pieces of track

☐ **MATERIALS**
Parts for the track system (see illustration), plastic anchors, screws, wire nuts, and electrician's tape

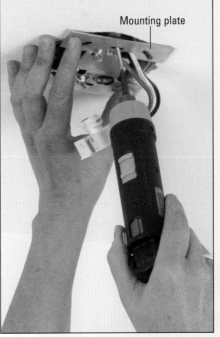
Mounting plate

**1** **Shut off power to the circuit** and remove the existing light fixture *(page 84)*. Splice the mounting plate leads to the house wires—green to ground, white to white, and black to black. Fold the wires up into the box. Screw the mounting plate snugly to the box.

**2** If necessary, cut pieces of track to length. To cut a track, hold it firmly in place. If you use a vice, take care not to bend the metal. Cut with a hacksaw that has a metal-cutting blade. Support the waste side of the piece when nearing the end of a cut so it does not fall and bend the track.

**TRACK LIGHTING SYSTEM**

*The mounting plate live-end connector supplies power to the track, which carries power via two strips of wire to the lamps.*

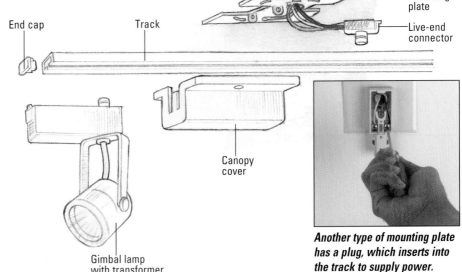

Box

Mounting plate

Live-end connector

End cap

Track

Canopy cover

Gimbal lamp with transformer

*Another type of mounting plate has a plug, which inserts into the track to supply power.*

# Installing track lights *(continued)*

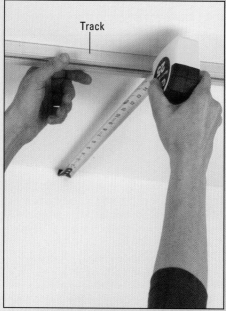

Track

**3** With a helper holding one end of the track, push the track up against the mounting plate. Secure it by tightening the setscrews.

**4** With a helper holding one end of the track, measure at two points along the track so it is parallel to the nearest wall. If the track configuration includes any 90-degree angles, use a framing square to mark a guide line.

**5** Locate joists with a stud finder. Drive a screw into every joist the track crosses. If the track runs parallel to the joists, drill holes every 16 inches, tap in plastic anchors, and drive screws into the anchors.

**TRACK CONFIGURATIONS**

*With various lamp directions and types of bulbs, track lighting can supply general illumination, task lighting, or accent lighting.*

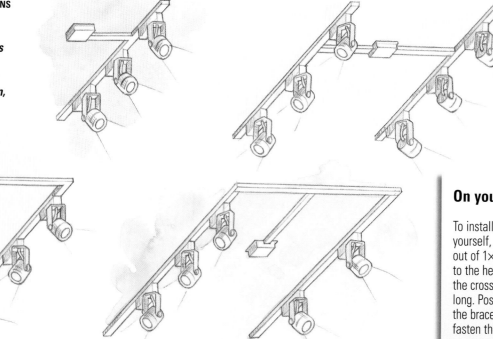

## On your own

To install track lighting by yourself, make two T-braces out of 1×2s. Cut the uprights to the height of the ceiling, the cross pieces about 2-feet long. Position the track, wedge the braces underneath, and fasten the track to the ceiling.

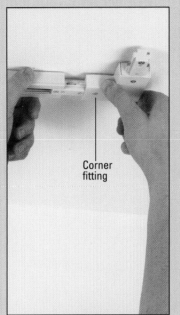

Live-end connector

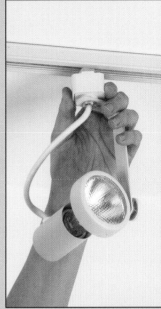

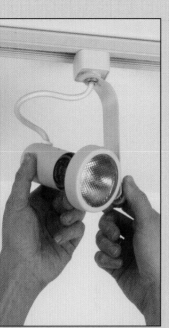

Corner fitting

**6** If the track has to turn a corner, slide the fitting onto the track piece just installed. Slide the next piece onto the connector, measure to see that it is parallel to the nearest wall, and anchor it to the ceiling.

**7** Once all the pieces are installed, place end caps on all the track ends. Push the live-end connector plug into the track; twist it to make contact with both strips of metal in the track. Attach the canopy cover.

**8** Insert the plug of a lamp into the track and twist to tighten. To move a lamp along the track, loosen it first—do not force it while it is still attached.

**9** Restore power and test. If a lamp does not work, remove it and twist it back on again. Once it works, adjust the lamp to direct the light where needed.

**FITTINGS**
## Any shape you need

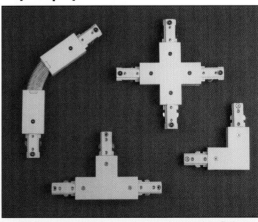

In addition to the "L" fitting *shown above,* other fittings allow you to form different shapes. A flexible fitting turns to most any angle. With each fitting you use, make sure the exposed ends of all the tracks have end caps, or the track will not energize.

## Available lamps

Incandescent bell lamp

Incandescent cylinder lamp

Halogen gimbal lamp

Swivel halogen lamp

Cylinder and bell lamps partially hide the bulb, while gimbal rings let them hang out. Low-voltage halogen lamps use less energy, but are expensive and become hot when they're on.

# CEILING FAN BOX

**C**eiling fans are heavy, and they vibrate. So if one is connected to a standard electrical box, there is a good chance that it will come loose and perhaps come crashing down.

The first step in adding a ceiling fan is to check out the existing electrical box. **Shut off power to the circuit,** and remove the existing ceiling fixture *(page 84).* Test to confirm that the power is off.

Most building codes require ceiling fans to be mounted onto special fan-rated boxes (opposite), which are made of metal or strong plastic and have deep threaded holes for the mounting screws. The box must be mounted firmly, either by attaching it directly to a framing member or by using a fan-rated brace *(Step 1, page 93).*

Replacing a ceiling box is a messy job. Work carefully to avoid cutting through wires hidden in the ceiling.

## PRESTART CHECKLIST

☐ **TIME**
About two hours to remove an old ceiling box and install a new one

☐ **TOOLS**
Screwdriver, hammer, drill, pry bar, flashlight, wrench or channel-lock pliers, and perhaps a reciprocating saw

☐ **SKILLS**
Cutting drywall, prying boxes out without damaging surrounding ceiling or wall

☐ **PREP**
Spread a drop cloth on the floor below and set up a ladder

☐ **MATERIALS**
Fan-rated box, box brace

## Remove old box

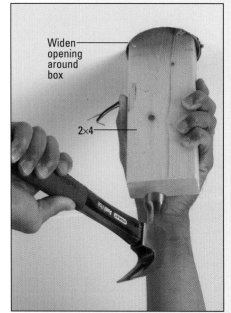

**1** Use a knife (not a saw) to cut through the drywall or plaster all around the old box. The box will be attached to a joist with screws or two horizontally driven nails. Force the box loose by hammering a 2×4 into it.

**2** Insert a flat pry bar between the box and the joist. Pry the box away from the joist. You may need to pry out a staple anchoring the cable to the joist. Work carefully to avoid unnecessary damage to the ceiling.

WHAT IF...
### There is another type of box in the ceiling?

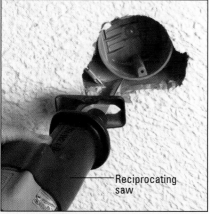

Older pancake boxes are mounted with screws driven into a framing member. Remove the screws and pry out the box.

If a box is too firmly mounted to be knocked free, cut a hole in the ceiling just large enough so you can see the mounting nails and the cable. Carefully cut through the nails with a reciprocating saw.

# Install new box

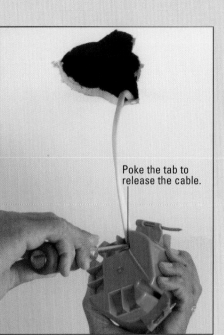

**3** Pry out the box's mounting nails and pull the box down from the ceiling. Disconnect the cable from the box. The box shown has a slot that the cable slides through; pry the tab and pull the cable out. If the box has a cable clamp, remove the locknut *(page 86)*.

Poke the tab to release the cable.

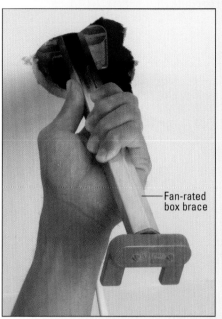

Fan-rated box brace

**1** To install a braced box, slip the brace through the hole. Rotate the shaft of the brace clockwise until it touches a joist on either side, and its legs rest on top of the drywall or plaster.

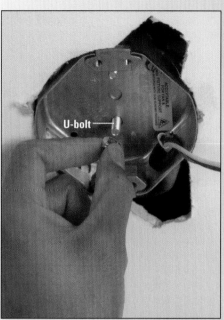

U-bolt

**2** Tighten the brace with a wrench or channel-lock pliers. Attach the U-bolt to the brace and slide the box up through it. Tighten the nuts.

## Available fan boxes

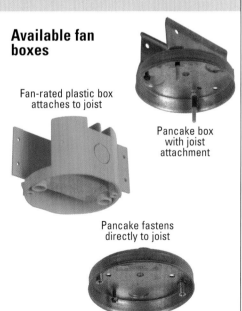

Fan-rated plastic box attaches to joist

Pancake box with joist attachment

Pancake fastens directly to joist

If a strong framing member is positioned directly above the box's hole, a pancake fan box or a box with a joist bracket through its center may be the easiest to install.

### WHAT IF...
## You can work from above?

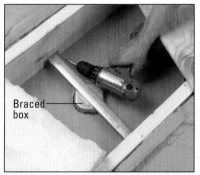

Braced box

If you can get at the attic space above the ceiling box, go there to disconnect the old box. Install a braced box.

**Don't depend on plaster lath:** If you have a plaster ceiling, make sure you attach a box to a joist—not the ⅜-inch-thick pieces of lath, which have very little strength.

## Screw the fan plate to a ceiling joist

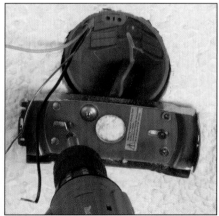

Here's an option that eliminates the need for a new box. Screw the fan's mounting plate *(page 94)* directly to a nearby joist. The plate will be off center, so you may need a medallion *(page 85)* to cover the hole.

# CEILING FAN

**A**lthough a ceiling fan is a complex fixture with lots of parts, each step of installation is fairly simple. The most challenging task is assembling the parts in the right order.

Make sure your ceiling box is fan-rated and strongly attached to framing *(pages 92–93)*.

If there is three-wire cable (with black, white, red, and ground wires) running from the fixture box to the switch box, you can install a standard fan/light switch *(page 96)*.

With two-wire cable (see *page 23* for the wiring possibilities), use one of the following means of controlling the fan and the light:
■ Have the wall switch control both the fan and the light; turn one or the other off using the fixture's pull-chain switches.
■ Install a wireless remote-control switch for the fan *(page 95)*.
■ Purchase a fan that has a special fan/light switch that works with two-wire cable (these are expensive).

## PRESTART CHECKLIST

☐ **TIME**
About 4 hours to install a ceiling fan and switch

☐ **TOOLS**
Screwdriver, drill, strippers, voltage tester, lineman's pliers, and a nonconducting ladder

☐ **SKILLS**
Stripping wire and splicing stranded wire to solid wire

☐ **PREP**
Spread a drop cloth on the floor below, position a ladder

☐ **MATERIALS**
Ceiling fan, wire nuts, and electrician's tape

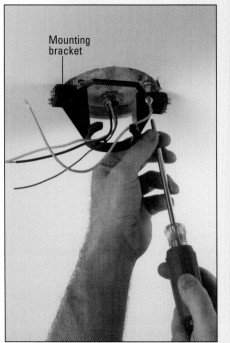

**1** **Test that there is no power in the box.** Secure the fan mounting bracket to the ceiling fixture box with screws. If rubber washers are provided, be sure to install them between the bracket and the box.

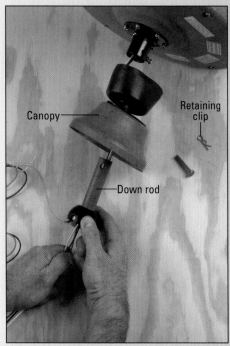

**2** Slide the down rod through the canopy, slip on the decorative cover, and pull the wires through. Slip the down rod over the fan housing and fasten with the retaining clip. Tighten the assembly.

**CEILING FAN**

*In this typical arrangement, the down rod and ball hanger nest in the mounting bracket, so it can vibrate without shaking the bracket. If you want the fan to hang down farther, purchase a down rod extender.*

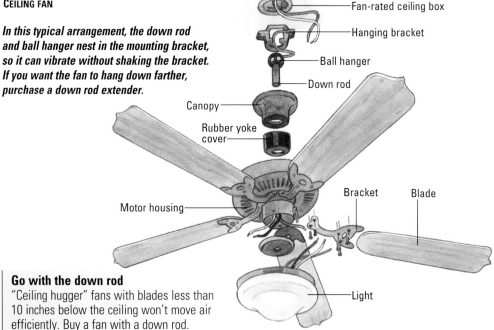

**Go with the down rod**
"Ceiling hugger" fans with blades less than 10 inches below the ceiling won't move air efficiently. Buy a fan with a down rod.

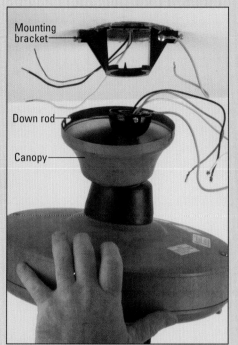

Mounting bracket

Down rod

Canopy

Fan blade

Canopy setscrew

Fan bracket

Cordless drill with phillips bit

**3** Carefully lift the assembled fan and hook the ball-like end of the down rod into the mounting bracket. Don't allow wires to get caught between the brackets and the end of the down rod. This ball and socket arrangement lets the fan unit swing slightly.

**4** Wire the fan. The black lead controls the motor and the blue or striped lead controls the light. If you have two-wire cable, splice both to the black house wire. Splice white lead to white wire and connect the grounds.

**5** Fold the wires into the box. Push the canopy against the ceiling and secure it to the mounting bracket with the setscrews provided. Screw a fan bracket onto each fan blade. Attach each fan bracket to the underside of the motor. Make sure all the screws are tight.

### Wireless remote control

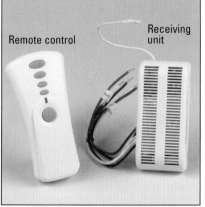

Remote control

Receiving unit

A wireless remote-control fan/light switch controls both the fan and the light from anywhere in the room. It has two parts. Wire the receiving unit according to its instructions and tuck it inside the canopy. The sending unit is battery-powered.

### Fan light options

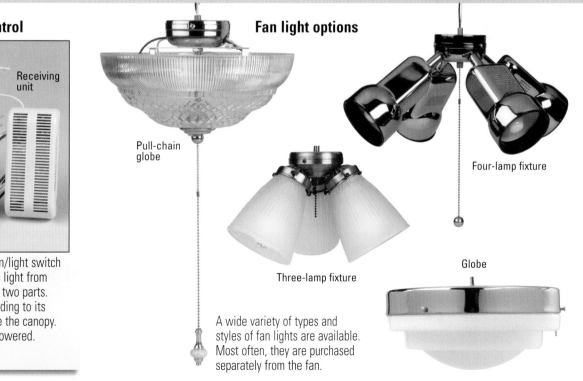

Pull-chain globe

Three-lamp fixture

Four-lamp fixture

Globe

A wide variety of types and styles of fan lights are available. Most often, they are purchased separately from the fan.

## Ceiling fan *(continued)*

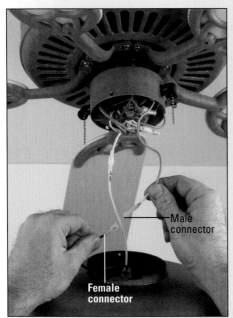

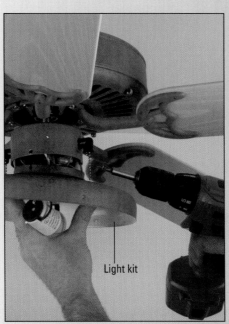

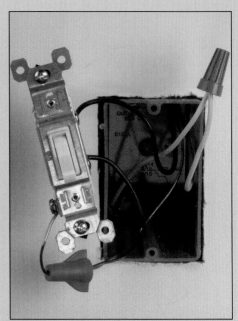

Male connector

Female connector

Light kit

**6** Remove the plate on the bottom of the fan and wire the light kit. The model shown above uses plug-together connectors. Some fans require that wires be spliced.

**7** Tuck the wires into the housing and push the light kit onto the fan. Tighten the screws to secure it. Install the lightbulb(s) and globe.

**8** In this arrangement, a standard single-pole switch turns the fan and the light on and off at the same time. To turn one or the other off, use the pull-chain switch. Do not install a standard dimmer for a fan—it will damage the fan.

---

### Fan switch options

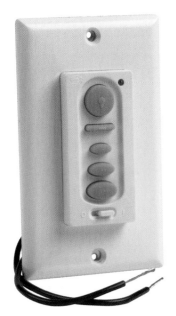

If you installed a fan only with no light kit, a push button fan control *(left)* operates the fan at different speeds.

With more expensive ceiling fans, switches are available that have separate controls for the fan and the light, though they require only two-wire cable.

**STANLEY** PRO TIP

#### Balancing the fan

If the fan wobbles, check the blade bracket screws and tighten if needed. Measure down from the ceiling to each blade; replace any that are warped. If that doesn't solve the problem, remove the blades and turn on the motor. If it wobbles without the blades, make sure the down rod is assembled correctly. If the fan still wobbles, purchase a fan balancing kit, which uses small weights to evenly distribute the load. Finally, the motor itself may be defective and may need to be replaced.

WHAT IF...
#### There is three-wire cable?

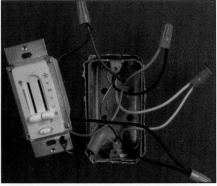

In this configuration, two-wire cable brings power into the switch box, and three-wire cable runs from the switch box to the fixture box. Connect the grounds. Splice the black lead to the black feed wire. Splice the light lead to the other black wire, and the fan lead to the red wire. Splice the white wires together.

# MOTION-SENSOR OUTDOOR LIGHT

For little more than the cost of a standard porch light, you can buy a light that turns on automatically when it senses movement. It can be installed on a wall or under an eaves.

Most models allow you to adjust how sensitive the light will be to movement, how long it stays on, and even how bright the light will be. If your existing porch light is controlled by an indoor switch, the motion-sensor light you install in its place can be controlled either by the switch or by the sensor.

## PRESTART CHECKLIST

☐ **TIME**
About two hours to remove the old light and install a motion-sensor light (wait until dark to adjust the light)

☐ **TOOLS**
Screwdriver, strippers, voltage tester, lineman's pliers, and a nonconducting ladder

☐ **SKILLS**
Stripping wire and splicing stranded wire to solid wire, mounting a fixture to a box

☐ **PREP**
Position a ladder so you can easily reach the existing light

☐ **MATERIALS**
*Motion-sensor light,* wire nuts, and electrician's tape

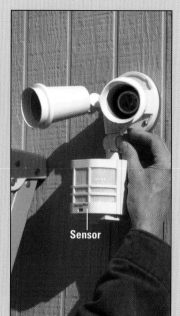

**1** **Shut off power to the circuit.** Remove the old fixture. Use the mounting bracket provided or install a swivel strap *(pages 84–85).* Some manufacturers provide a bracket to suspend the fixture temporarily while you splice the wires.

**2** Mount the light using the screws provided. Position the rubber gasket to provide a watertight seal. Slip the mounting screws through their holes in the fixture and drive them into the holes in the bracket or strap.

**3** Loosen each flood light's locknut, swivel the light to the desired position, and tighten the locknut. Point the sensor toward where you expect motion. After dark, test the light and make adjustments.

**EAVES-MOUNTED MOTION-SENSOR OUTDOOR LIGHT**

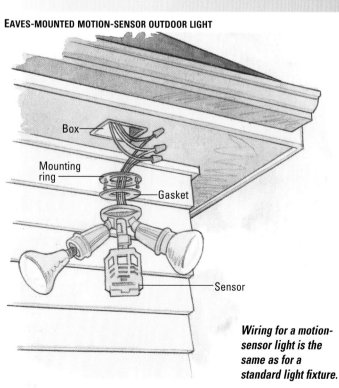

*Wiring for a motion-sensor light is the same as for a standard light fixture.*

## MAKE ADJUSTMENTS
### Range of motion

Controls are located on an adjustment panel. Point the sensor and set sensitivity (RANGE) to the middle position. Test to see that people approaching the house will turn on the light, but not neighbors walking by. Redirect the sensor or adjust the sensitivity if necessary. Also adjust how long the light will stay on (ON TIME).

# WIRING LOW-VOLTAGE PROJECTS

Thermostats, telephones, door chimes, and some (but not all) halogen fixtures use wires that carry very small amounts of electricity—in most cases, from 8 to 20 volts. You can touch these wires while they are live and feel only a pinprick of a shock. There is no need to shut off power before performing an installation or repair. Use a multitester to **check the voltage** in the wires before you begin any work.

Some halogen fixtures (such as track lights) are connected to standard-voltage wiring; a transformer inside the fixture steps current down. Be sure to **turn power off** before working on one of these.

### Finding the transformer

Low-voltage wiring (other than phone line) is usually connected to a transformer, which reduces 120-volt household current to a mere trickle. In some fixtures the transformer is built into the fixture canopy. Other transformers are separate units attached to junction boxes, located in out-of-the-way areas such as a garage, crawlspace, basement, or cabinet. Some units have transformers that plug into standard electrical receptacles *(pages 100–101)*.

Follow the low-voltage wires carefully to locate the transformer. All 120-volt connections to the transformers should be enclosed in a junction box; only the connections for the thin, low-voltage wires can be left exposed.

### Protecting the cord

Low-voltage cord or cable has only a thin plastic sheathing, so the wires can be easily nicked or sliced by a wayward fastener. Keep low-voltage wiring out of harm's way. Hide it when possible. When it must be exposed, staple it carefully.

Coaxial cable for cable TV is often installed poorly and may droop lower than 8 feet above your yard. Insist that the cable company rectify this hazard by moving the cable up and fastening it firmly or by burying it.

## Low-voltage units connect easily and pose a reduced hazard of shock.

### CHAPTER PREVIEW

**Undercabinet lights**
*page 100*

**Euro-style halogen lights**
*page 102*

**Low-voltage outdoor lights**
*page 104*

**Repairing a door chime**
*page 106*

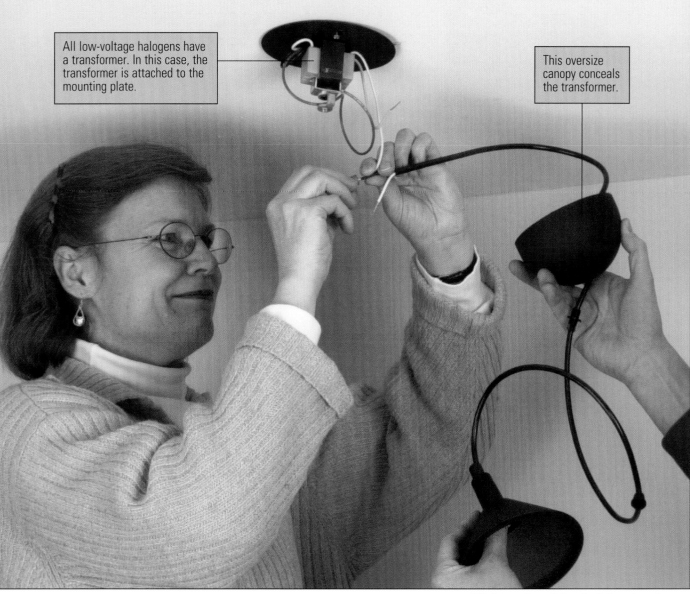

All low-voltage halogens have a transformer. In this case, the transformer is attached to the mounting plate.

This oversize canopy conceals the transformer.

*This low-voltage fixture includes a transformer, which is attached to the ceiling box (above). It reduces voltage from 120 volts to just 12 volts. Installation is easy: once the transformer is secure, the wires can be spliced and the canopy fastened in place. Enlist a helper to hold a ceiling fixture while installing it; the wiring connections are not intended to support the weight of the light.*

**Wall-mounted stereo speakers**
*page 109*

**TV cable**
*page 110*

**Thermostats**
*page 112*

**Phone lines**
*page 113*

# Undercabinet Lights

The easiest way to light up counter space is to install low-voltage halogen lights on the underside of wall cabinets. Halogens can also help create a dramatic display area inside glass-fronted cabinets.

The most common type of halogen is called a puck light because of its shape, but other shapes are available. Buy a kit that includes lights, cord, a transformer, and a cord switch. Some models allow you to hook up several more lights, if needed.

Halogens get very hot. Locate them out of children's reach or where they won't be accidentally touched. In areas where heat can build up—such as inside a cabinet—install bulbs of lower wattage.

Plan the locations of the lights and the plug-in unit and work out the least conspicuous route for the cord. Either staple the cord under a cabinet or shelf, or drill small holes and run the cord inside the cabinets and out of sight.

If you want to control halogens from a wall switch, install a switch/receptacle (page 101).

**1** Position each lighting unit as recommended by the manufacturer. Check that the mounting screws provided won't pierce through to the inside of the cabinet. Fasten each fixture in place.

Plug-in halogen light

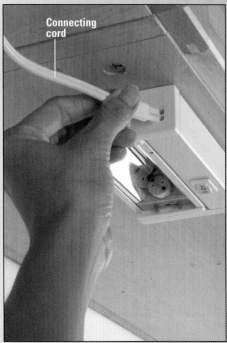

Connecting cord

**2** When all the fixtures are in place, run connecting wires between them; then connect the source line that runs from the lights to a receptacle. Some kits come with plugs already installed. Coil any excess wire and hide it near the back of the cabinet.

## Prestart Checklist

□ **Time**
About two hours to install five or six halogens with transformer and switch

□ **Tools**
Screwdriver, drill, strippers, stapler, and a hammer

□ **Skills**
Drilling holes and driving screws

□ **Prep**
Spread a towel or small drop cloth on the surface below

□ **Materials**
Halogen light kit, including lights, a plug-in unit, transformer, cord, and switch

**INSTALLING UNDERCABINET PUCK LIGHTS**

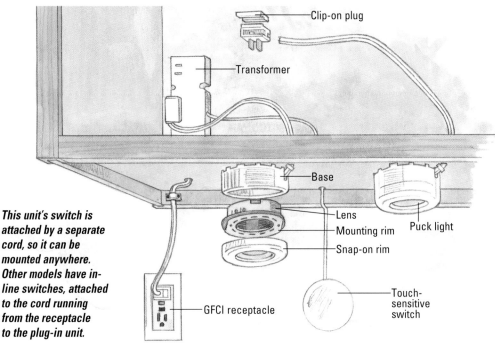

*This unit's switch is attached by a separate cord, so it can be mounted anywhere. Other models have in-line switches, attached to the cord running from the receptacle to the plug-in unit.*

Clip-on plug

Transformer

Base

Lens

Mounting rim

Puck light

Snap-on rim

GFCI receptacle

Touch-sensitive switch

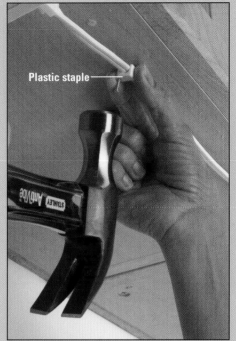

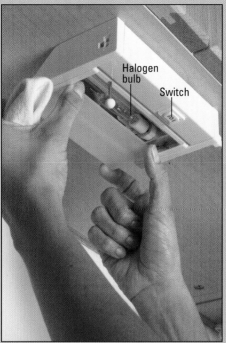

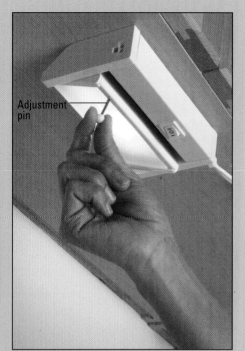

**3** Fasten the connecting cords to the underside of the cabinet. Use the staples provided with the kit, or plastic-coated or round-topped staples. Don't use standard metal square-topped staples; they may cut the cord.

**4** Slide back the lens covering. Holding the halogen bulb with a cloth, install it in the fixture. Replace the lens.

**5** Plug in the main cord and turn the lights on with the switch. On the model shown above, the direction of the lamp can be adjusted by holding an attached pin and swiveling the lamp housing.

**STANLEY** PRO TIP: **Wiring a switch/receptacle**

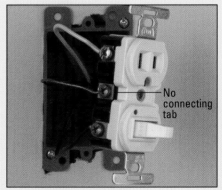

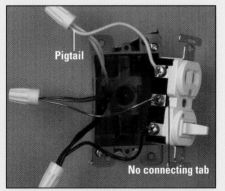

**Shut off the power.** Remove the old receptacle *(page 75)*. Connect the grounds *(page 38)*. Connect the black wire to the brass terminal that does not have a connecting tab and connect the white wire to the silver terminal on the same side. The switch will turn the receptacle on and off.

If the receptacle is in the middle of the run, with two cables entering the box *(page 75)*, splice the black wires and the white wires to pigtails and connect them to the brass and silver terminals on the side that does not have a connecting tab.

**Rope lights**

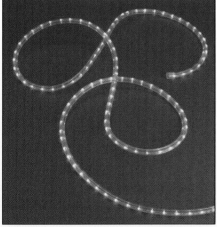

Rope lights are especially easy to install. Just staple them where you want them, using the plastic staples supplied, and plug them in. Install an in-line cord switch *(page 55)*, or plug into a switched receptacle *(left)*.

# Euro-Style Halogen Lights

**H**igh-tech-looking Euro-style lights are readily available at lighting stores and home centers. They look complicated, but they are easy to install.

Use one of these fixtures to replace an existing light fixture, as shown on these pages, or buy a unit that simply can be plugged into a receptacle.

Low-voltage halogens save on energy use. But halogen bulbs get very hot, so keep them out of the reach of children and well away from combustible surfaces, such as curtains.

The fixture uses a transformer that steps voltage down—typically to 8 to 20 volts. However, you will be hooking it up to standard household wiring, so be sure to **shut off power** before working. To remove an existing light fixture, see *page 84*.

## Prestart Checklist

☐ **Time**
About two hours to remove a ceiling fixture and install a Euro-style light

☐ **Tools**
Screwdriver, drill, voltage tester, stud finder, strippers, lineman's pliers, and a nonconducting ladder

☐ **Skills**
Attaching hardware with screws, stripping wire, splicing stranded wire to solid wire

☐ **Prep**
Spread a drop cloth on the floor below.

☐ **Materials**
New light fixture, wire nuts, and electrician's tape

Transformer

Canopy

**1** **Shut off power to the circuit.** Remove an existing light fixture *(page 84)* and splice the transformer leads to the house wires.

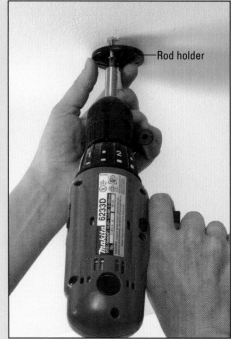

Rod holder

**2** Measure carefully and try to position the rod holders under a joist. Attach the holders with screws long enough to reach through drywall or plaster and fasten at least ½ inch into the joist. Use plastic wall anchors if no joist is available.

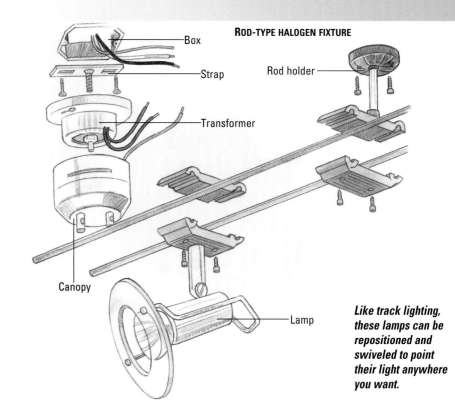

**Rod-Type Halogen Fixture**

Box

Strap

Rod holder

Transformer

Canopy

Lamp

*Like track lighting, these lamps can be repositioned and swiveled to point their light anywhere you want.*

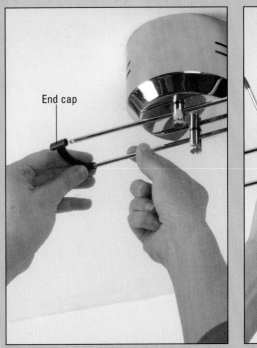

End cap

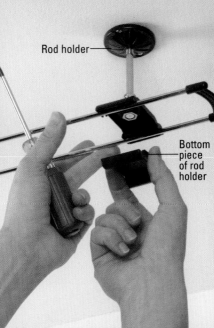

Rod holder

Bottom piece of rod holder

**3** Mount the transformer and canopy to the ceiling box strap *(page 84)*. Slide the rods through the canopy rod connectors. Slip an end cap onto the two rods at either end.

**4** Remove the bottom piece from each rod holder, snap the rods up into the grooves, and screw the bottom piece back into place.

**5** Attach each lamp the same way that you clamped the rods to the rod holders. Slide the lamp into position before completely tightening the screw.

## Stylish options

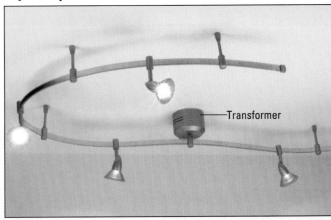

Transformer

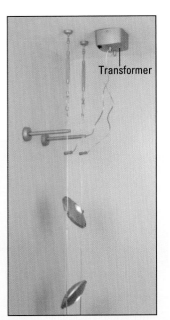

Transformer

With a track that can be bent into curves, the halogen fixture (above) is as decorative as it is functional. The transformer can be mounted anywhere along the track, and the track can be cut to any desired length. Lights straddle two vertical wires (right), which deliver low-voltage current. Lights can slide up or down and rotate on an axis. The same unit can be installed horizontally.

**REFRESHER COURSE**
### Switch/receptacle for plug-in transformers

If you have no existing ceiling fixture, buy a unit that plugs into a receptacle. *Page 74* shows how to replace a receptacle with a switched plug, so you can control the light with a wall switch.

# LOW-VOLTAGE OUTDOOR LIGHTS

Low-voltage outdoor lights simply poke into the ground with stakes. The cable can be hidden under ground cover, buried in a shallow trench, or covered lightly with soil or mulch. If there is an outdoor receptacle, attach the transformer nearby and plug it in. To connect cable to a light, snap together components.

Plan carefully before installing outdoor lights. Make a drawing of your property, including plants and structures. Choose from a variety of light fixtures: tiered or flower-shaped lights to mark a pathway, floodlights to accentuate foliage or provide security, and deck lights to illuminate vertical surfaces such as step risers.

Add up the wattage of the lights you want to use and choose a transformer/timer that will supply enough power. For instance, eight 18-watt lights and five 20-watt lights add up to 244 watts. A 250-watt transformer will handle the load, but you will not have the option of adding lights in the future—so you may want to buy a larger transformer.

## PRESTART CHECKLIST

☐ **TIME**
About 4 hours to install 10 to 15 lights and cover the cable

☐ **TOOLS**
Screwdriver, lineman's pliers, hammer, gardening trowel, and perhaps a drill

☐ **SKILLS**
Stripping and splicing wires

☐ **PREP**
If there is no outdoor receptacle, have one installed. Or plug the transformer into an indoor receptacle and drill a small hole for the cable to run through to the outside.

☐ **MATERIALS**
Low-voltage outdoor light kit, including lights, transformer/timer and cable (you may buy additional lights and cable)

**1** Insert the tip of each lamp stake into the ground and push it in. If the soil is hard, first cut a slit with a gardening trowel, then push in the stake.

**2** Run the cord from the house receptacle to each of the lamps. Hide the cord under ground cover, dig a shallow trench for the cord, or cover it with mulch. On a deck or porch, staple the cord where it will be out of sight.

**INSTALLING LOW-VOLTAGE OUTDOOR LIGHTS**

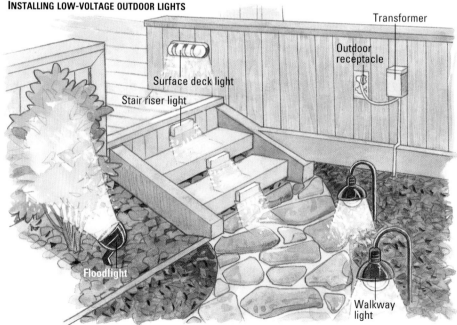

Transformer

Outdoor receptacle

Surface deck light

Stair riser light

Floodlight

Walkway light

*This system combines several types of lights. The cable is run in a shallow trench in the ground or stapled to the house or deck.*

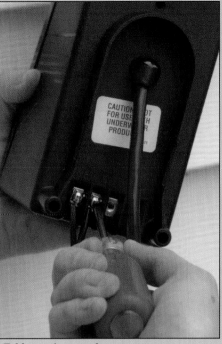

**3** To connect a light to power, slip the two parts of its connector around the cord and snap them together. They'll pierce and pinch the cord to make the connection.

Snap-on connector

**4** Mount the transformer near a receptacle, where it will stay dry and won't be damaged. Strip the cord's wire ends and connect them to the transformer terminals, following the manufacturer's instructions.

**5** Plug in the transformer. Most models turn lights on automatically when it gets dark and give you the option of setting the lights on a timer. Follow manufacturer's instructions for programming.

## WHAT IF...
### There is a HI/LO switch?

A HI/LO switch allows you to boost the power to the lights. First, try running the lights with the switch set to LO. If some lights do not come on, or if they are too dim, flip the switch to HI.

## REFRESHER COURSE
### Use a GFCI outdoors

Any receptacle that is exposed to moisture should be a GFCI. To replace a standard receptacle with a GFCI, **shut off power** to the circuit, remove the old receptacle, and restrip the wire ends. If only one cable enters the box, connect the wires to the LINE terminals. If two cables enter the box, connect the wires that bring power into the box to the LINE terminals, and connect the other wires to the LOAD terminals. See *page 76* for more instructions.

## Solar light

Solar-powered lights are easy to install. Just push them into the ground; no wiring is required. Solar lights are handy for spots far away from a power source. The location must receive at least three or four hours of sunlight a day to provide light at night. It generally takes a few days for the battery to build up power. A solar light may not work well during prolonged periods of cloudy weather.

# REPAIRING A DOOR CHIME

If a chime or bell does not sound when you push the button, follow the steps shown on these pages: Check the button first, then the chime, then the transformer.

All these components are easily repaired or replaced. However, if the wiring is damaged inside walls, replacing it can be very difficult.

Power for a doorbell is supplied by a transformer, usually attached to a metal electrical box in some out-of-the-way location, such as a basement, crawlspace, garage, or inside a cabinet. Work carefully—other components, such as thermostats, might have similar-looking transformers. Follow the wires to be sure.

Doorbell wires may be color-coded, but there is no predicting which color goes to which button. Often, all the wires are the same color.

Because the bell circuit operates on low voltage, you do not need to turn off power while testing the button or chime. However, the transformer is connected to 120 volts. **Shut off power** before working on the transformer.

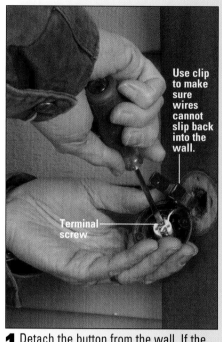

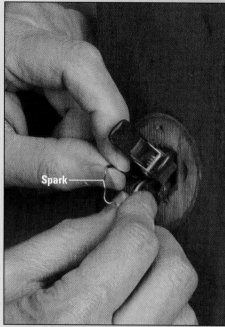

Use clip to make sure wires cannot slip back into the wall.

Terminal screw

Spark

**1** Detach the button from the wall. If the mounting screws are not visible, you may need to snap off a cover to reach them. To remove a small round button, pry it out with a screwdriver. Clean away any debris. Make sure wires are not broken. Tighten terminal screws.

**2** If that does not solve the problem, detach the wires from the terminals. Hold each wire by its insulation and touch the bare wires together. If you get a tiny spark and the chime sounds, replace the button. If you get a spark and the chime does not sound, test the chime *(Step 4)*. If there is no spark, check the transformer *(Step 5)*.

## PRESTART CHECKLIST

☐ **TIME**
About two hours to diagnose and repair most problems, not including time spent buying the new part

☐ **TOOLS**
Screwdriver, strippers, perhaps a multitester

☐ **SKILLS**
Stripping wires, attaching wires to terminals, using multitester

☐ **MATERIALS**
Short length of wire, perhaps a new button, chime, or transformer

**SINGLE CHIME SYSTEM**

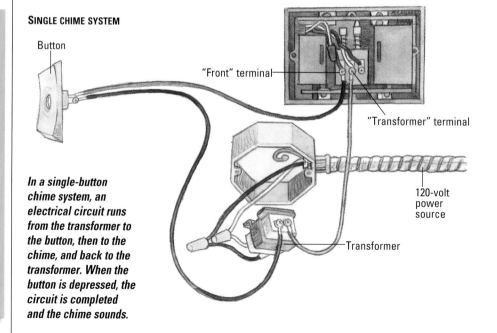

Button

"Front" terminal

"Transformer" terminal

120-volt power source

Transformer

*In a single-button chime system, an electrical circuit runs from the transformer to the button, then to the chime, and back to the transformer. When the button is depressed, the circuit is completed and the chime sounds.*

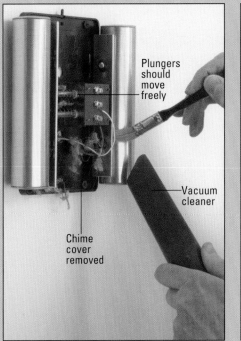

Plungers should move freely

Vacuum cleaner

Chime cover removed

Multitester

Transformer

**3** If a chime does not sound or has a muffled sound, remove the cover and clean any dust or gunk. Make sure the wires are firmly connected to the terminal screws. If there is corrosion on the connections, detach and clean the wires and terminals with steel wool or light sandpaper.

**4** Set a multitester to a low AC reading and touch the probes to "front" and "trans" terminals, then to "rear" and "trans." If you get a reading that is close to the chime's printed voltage rating, power is entering the chime. That indicates the chime mechanism is not functioning and needs replacing.

**5** If there is no power at the chime, test the transformer. Remove the thin wires. Touch the probes of the multitester to both terminals. If it reads more than 2 volts below the transformer's rating, replace the transformer.

## Wireless options

Wireless chime

Battery-powered button

Wireless add-on chime

Sending unit

A wireless chime installs easily. Put a battery in the button and attach it to the outside of the house. Then plug the chime into an electrical receptacle.

To add a second chime to your system, buy a wireless add-on chime. Place the sending unit inside the existing chime and connect its wires to the terminals. Plug the wireless chime into an electrical receptacle and mount it on the wall.

### CHIME NEEDS REPLACING
**Find a new chime with the same voltage rating**

Before removing a chime, tag the wires so you know where they go. Loosen the terminal screws and remove the wires. Remove the mounting screws. Pull the chime out, carefully threading the wires through the hole in the chime.

Purchase a new chime of the same voltage rating as the transformer. (The voltage rating is usually printed on the chime unit.) Make sure the chime housing is large enough to cover any imperfections in the wall. Slip the wires through the opening in the housing, mount it to the wall, and connect the wires.

# Repairing a door chime (continued)

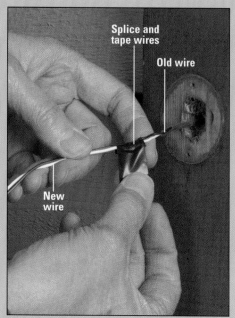

**6** Before you buy a new transformer, make sure the box it is attached to has power. If it's attached to a receptacle box, insert the tester probes in the receptacle slots. If it's attached to a junction box, carefully remove the cover and test the wires *(page 42)*. **Remember, these are 120-volt wires.**

**7** If the transformer doesn't work, buy a new one with the same voltage rating. **Shut off power** to the circuit. Open the box and disconnect the transformer wires. Remove the nut that clamps the transformer to the box and pull out the transformer. Wire and clamp the new transformer.

**8** If the transformer tests OK but no power reaches the chime or a button, the wiring is damaged. You may be able to attach new wire to the old and pull the new wire through. If you can't rewire, install a wireless chime *(page 107)*.

**TWO-CHIME SYSTEM**

*In a two-button system, a separate wire runs from the chime to the transformer to create a complete circuit for both buttons.*

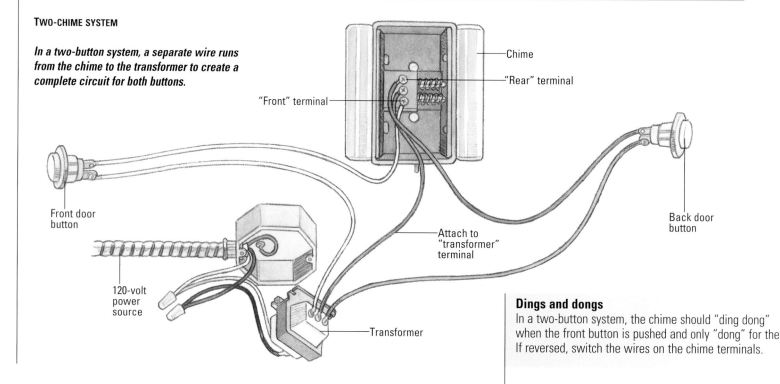

**Dings and dongs**
In a two-button system, the chime should "ding dong" when the front button is pushed and only "dong" for the If reversed, switch the wires on the chime terminals.

# WALL-MOUNTED STEREO SPEAKERS

**S**peaker wires often lie exposed on the floor, where they are both a nuisance and an eyesore. But there are several ways to tuck the wires out of sight.

Thin speaker wire may degrade the sound quality of a speaker, especially if the wire extends longer than 8 feet. Take no chances; buy wire that is #12 or thicker.

Speaker cord has two wires of different colors, or else one smooth and one ribbed wire. Be sure the connections are polarized. The wire attached to the receiver terminal labeled + or L should be connected to the + or L terminal on the speaker. The same goes for the - or R terminals.

## PRESTART CHECKLIST

☐ **TIME**
About two hours to install a wall speaker or hide speaker wire for two speakers

☐ **TOOLS**
Flat pry bar, screwdriver, drill, strippers, round-topped stapler, drywall saw

☐ **SKILLS**
Cutting holes in walls and prying off moldings

☐ **MATERIALS**
Speakers, speaker wire

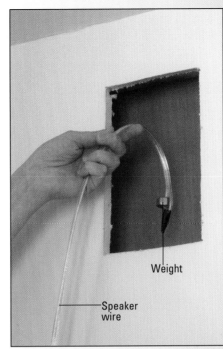
Weight
Speaker wire

Speaker

**1** Mark the wall using the measurements or template provided with the speakers. Cut the hole using a drywall saw. To run wire through a wall, attach a weight and drop it down. Cut or drill a small hole at the bottom of the wall, directly under the speaker hole. Fish the end of the wire out.

**2** Slip the speaker into the hole and drive the screws, which tighten the speaker's mounting flange to the wall. Snap the grill on and hook the speaker wire to the receiver.

**STANLEY** PRO TIP: **Hiding speaker wire**

Pry bar

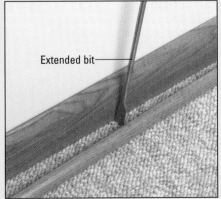
Extended bit

Pry the base mold out just far enough to slip the wire behind it. You may need to use a block of wood while prying to avoid damaging the wall.

Tap the molding back into place with a hammer and wood block. If needed, use a nail set to secure the nails.

Another option is to run the wire into the basement or a crawlspace. Pry away the base shoe and drill a hole with a long ½-inch bit. Use a straightened coat hanger to guide the wire down through the hole. Cut or sand a small notch for the wire in the base shoe, then nail it back into place.

# TV CABLE

Coaxial cable used for cable TV installations uses special male/female connectors and splitters. Twist-on connectors are available but do not provide as solid a connection as a crimp-on connector. You'll need a special crimping tool to work with those connectors (see below). For outdoor locations, use watertight connections—a standard connector or splitter will rust quickly. All are available at electronics or hardware stores.

Run cable into a low-voltage (LV) ring, which is like an electrical box without a back *(page 111)*.

Have the cable service provider do as much of the work of running the cable as possible. If service technicians run the cable in your house, provide specific instructions to route the cable, requesting that they adequately hide the cable. Or ask them to leave a coil of cable that you can install yourself.

## PRESTART CHECKLIST

☐ **TIME**
About 3 hours to install a splitter or two, run about 40 feet of cable, and install a jack

☐ **TOOLS**
Drill, long ½-inch bit, screwdriver, strippers, utility knife, crimping tool, and a drywall saw

☐ **SKILLS**
Stripping cable, running cable through walls or behind moldings

☐ **PREP**
Spread a towel or drop cloth below where you will cut the wall

☐ **MATERIALS**
RG6 coaxial cable, cable staples, male connectors, splitters, LV ring, wall jack

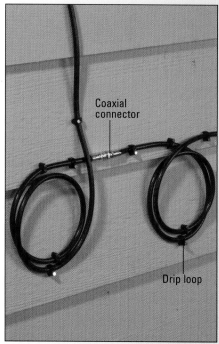

**1** Where the cable enters the house, there is a watertight metal connector, or possibly a splitter, and a "drip loop" that carries water away from the connector. To split the line outside rather than inside, ask the cable company to provide the fitting and the cable.

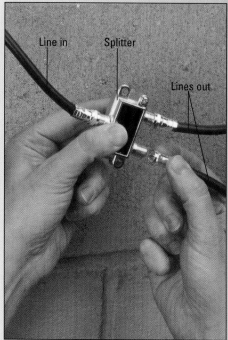

**2** To split a line, cut the existing line at a convenient location. Make male ends on both cuts and on the new line *(below)*. Screw the three male ends into a splitter and attach it to a wall or joist with screws. If you're attaching to masonry, drill holes and use plastic anchors with screws.

**STANLEY** PRO TIP: **Making the male end**

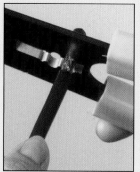

**1** Strip ½ inch of outer sheathing. With a knife, cut just barely through the sheathing—don't cut through the wire mesh that lies inside. Pull the sheathing off with your fingers.

**2** Push back the wire mesh. Strip ⅜ inch of plastic insulation from the center wire end. Slip a crimp-on connector on the cable end. Push until the wire protrudes beyond the front of the connector by about ¹⁄₁₆ inch.

**3** With a special coaxial crimping tool (don't try to use pliers), squeeze the connector sleeve tightly onto the cable.

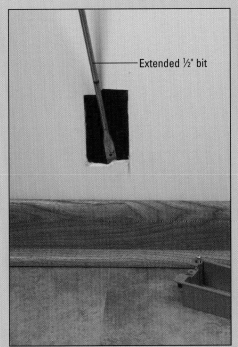

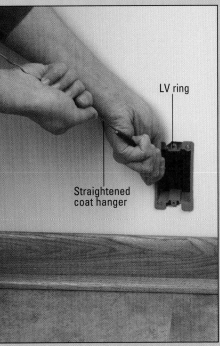

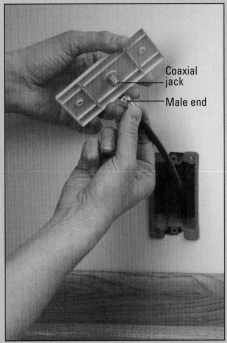

**3** To run cable up from a basement or crawlspace, cut a hole in the wall to accommodate a low-voltage (LV) ring *(Step 4)*. With an extended ½-inch bit, drill a hole down through the floor inside the wall.

**4** Insert an LV ring into the hole and tighten the mounting screws. Poke a hanger wire down through the hole in the floor; from below, attach the end of the cable to the hanger wire with tape. Pull the cable up through the holes.

**5** Make a male end on the cable *(page 110)* and screw it tightly to the back of a coaxial wall jack. Screw the jack to the LV ring.

## Antenna alternatives

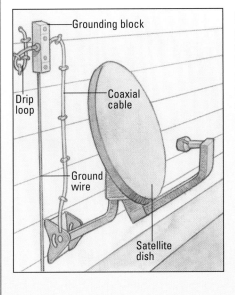

Some satellite dishes are suitable for do-it-yourself installation. From a grounding block, run RG6 cable down an exterior wall, staple it in place with plastic staples, and connect it to the dish. Attach a grounded copper wire to the grounding block. Run the ground wire to a grounding stake *(page 19)*. Make a drip loop where the cable enters the house. Inside, run the cable to a wall jack and plug the dish receiver into the jack. Follow manufacturer's instructions for pointing the dish.

Even with a satellite dish, an old-fashioned TV antenna may be needed to receive local channels. Some antennas have a coaxial connection. Others have a twin-wire lead. Use an adapter, available from an electronics store or home center, to connect a twin-wire antenna lead to coaxial cable.

## The right cable

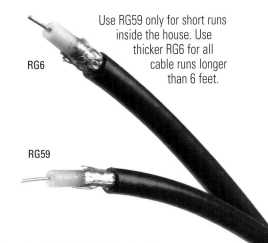

Use RG59 only for short runs inside the house. Use thicker RG6 for all cable runs longer than 6 feet.

**Fuzzy reception?**
If reception is fuzzy on one or more TVs, inspect all the splices and tighten if needed. If the problem continues, ask the cable company about having a signal amplifier installed.

# THERMOSTATS

A thermostat senses when the air temperature is a degree or two above or below the desired level and switches the heating or cooling system on or off accordingly.

If a thermostat is attached to an electrical box and has standard house wires connected to it, it is a line-voltage unit. If it malfunctions, **shut off power to the circuit**, remove it, and take it to a dealer for a replacement.

A low-voltage thermostat like the one shown here receives power from a transformer, much like that for a door chime. The transformer is typically located on or near the heating or cooling unit. Replace the transformer if it does not deliver power *(pages 107–108)*. In a typical setup, two wires control the heater and two control the air conditioner. If there are more wires, consult a heating and cooling pro.

## PRESTART CHECKLIST

☐ **TIME**
Less than an hour for most repairs

☐ **TOOLS**
Screwdriver, soft brush, and strippers

☐ **SKILLS**
Stripping wire, making connections

☐ **MATERIALS**
Short length of thin-gauge wire, and perhaps a replacement thermostat or transformer

**1** On a low-voltage thermostat, pull off the outer cover and loosen screws to remove the inner cover. Clean away dust with a soft brush. Gently lift the control lever and clean the contact beneath it. Replace the covers and test.

**2** If it still doesn't work, test for power. Strip the ends of a short wire and touch the terminals marked W and R. If they spark and the heating unit comes on, the thermostat is broken and should be replaced. If nothing happens, check the transformer *(page 108)*.

WHAT IF ...
### The room temperature is far different from the setting?

If the thermostat is sending the wrong message to the heating unit or air conditioner, it may be out of plumb. Use a string with a small weight near the two alignment marks. If they do not line up, loosen the mounting screws and twist the thermostat.

**STANLEY** PRO TIP

### Installing a new thermostat

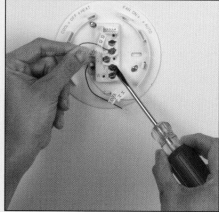

Replacing a thermostat is not difficult. Tag the wires before removing the old unit. Make sure the new thermostat is plumb *(see box at left)* and drive mounting screws. Attach the wires, inner cover, and outer cover.

# PHONE LINES

**D**elivering phone service to the house is the telephone company's business. For a fee, the phone company will also run lines and add jacks inside, but you'll save money—and get exactly what you want—doing it yourself.

Telephone wiring is straightforward, but running cable so it is hidden from view takes time and effort. Before running and stapling cable, plan the entire run. Extra effort may save trouble and eliminate an eyesore. For instance, running cable through a wall may mean that you do not have to run it around a door.

For easy and secure connections, buy telephone cable that has solid-core 24-gauge wire. Cheaper cables have stranded wires that are difficult to handle.

## PRESTART CHECKLIST

☐ **TIME**
About 3 hours to tap into a junction box, run cable, and install a jack

☐ **TOOLS**
Screwdriver, drill, strippers, lineman's pliers, phone tool *(page 114),* round-topped stapler, flat pry bar, stud finder, voltage detector, and drywall saw

☐ **SKILLS**
Stripping and connecting wires to terminals

☐ **PREP**
Find the best route for the phone wires; if possible, avoid having to go around a doorway

☐ **MATERIALS**
Telephone cable or Cat-5 cable, phone jacks, round-topped staples or plastic-coated staples

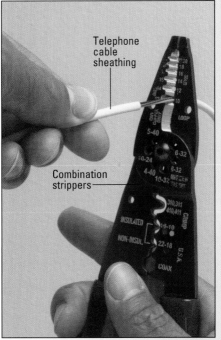
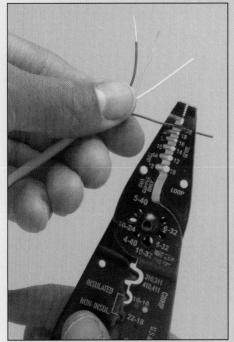

Telephone cable sheathing

Combination strippers

**1** To add an extension line, first loosen the screw and remove the cover from a convenient existing phone jack. Using strippers, remove about 2 inches of sheathing from the new cable using the 10 slot of the strippers.

**2** Strip about ½ inch from each wire using the 22/20 slot on the strippers. Loosen each terminal screw, remove the wire attached to it, and twist it together with the new wire of the same color.

**EXTENDING A TELEPHONE LINE**

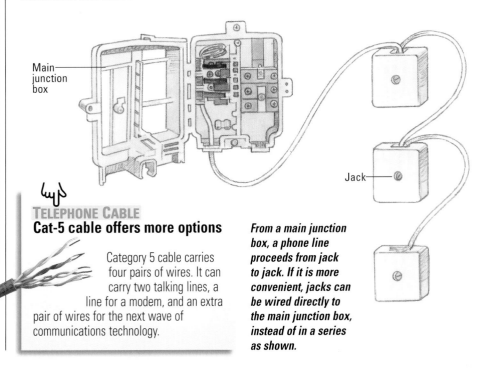

Main junction box

Jack

**TELEPHONE CABLE**
### Cat-5 cable offers more options

Category 5 cable carries four pairs of wires. It can carry two talking lines, a line for a modem, and an extra pair of wires for the next wave of communications technology.

*From a main junction box, a phone line proceeds from jack to jack. If it is more convenient, jacks can be wired directly to the main junction box, instead of in a series as shown.*

# Phone lines *(continued)*

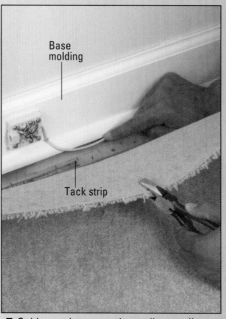

Base
molding

Tack strip

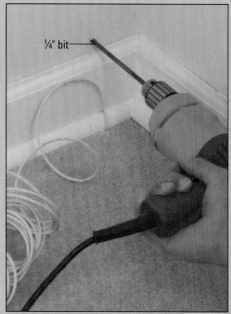

¼" bit

**3** Loop each pair of wires clockwise around their terminal screws. Tighten the screws and push the cable into the hole provided. You may have to snap out a breakout tab.

**4** Cable can be run under wall-to-wall carpeting. Use lineman's pliers to pull back a short section at a time and run the cable between the tack strip and the molding.

**5** To run cable through a wall, drill a hole through both sides of the wall using an extended ¼-inch drill bit. Use a stud finder to avoid running into a framing member. Use a voltage detector to check walls if electrical cable is present.

## Tapping into a junction box

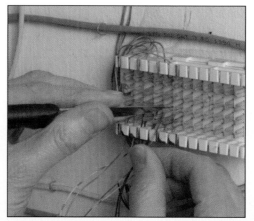

It may be easier to run cable discretely by starting at a junction box rather than a phone jack. Many houses have a junction box, like the one above, attached to the exterior. One section of the box is accessible to the homeowner; attach wires as you would in a phone jack *(Step 2)*.

An indoor junction box or phone jack may have slide-on connectors. Do not strip the wire. Slide the wire end down onto the metal slit, using a thin slot screwdriver or a dull knife.

**STANLEY** Pro Tip

### Running two or more lines using one cable

When installing a new line, it may be possible to piggyback on existing cable rather than running new cable. A phone line uses one pair of wires. With two-pair cable, the red and the green wires are used for the first line, and the yellow and black wires for the second. Three-pair cable, as well as four-pair Category 5 cable, are also available.

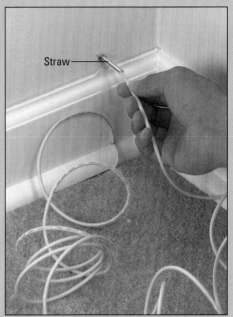

Straw

Staple

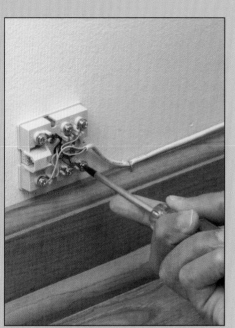

**6** Poke a long soda straw through the hole and fish it around until it pushes through the hole in the wall behind. Feed the cable through the straw. Remove the straw from the other side of the wall.

**7** If there is no carpeting to hide the line, staple it to the top of the base molding. Use round-topped staples or staples made specially for phone line.

**8** Attach a new jack to the base molding by drilling pilot holes and driving screws. To attach to a drywall or plaster wall, drill holes, insert plastic anchors, and drive screws into the anchors. Connect wires and attach cover.

## WHAT IF...
## A jack is needed for a wall-mounted phone?

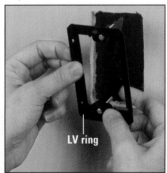

LV ring

Weight

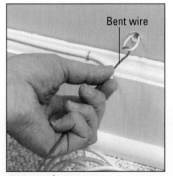

Bent wire

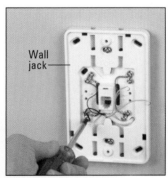

Wall jack

**1** Use a stud finder to make sure the opening won't overlap a stud. Cut a hole in drywall with a drywall saw. With plaster walls, cut with a utility knife first, then use a saber saw. Slip a low-voltage (LV) ring into the hole and tighten the screws to secure the ring to the drywall or plaster.

**2** Attach a small weight, such as a nut, to a string, and guide it down the hole until it hits bottom.

**3** Drill a ½-inch hole in the wall near the floor directly below the hole for the wall jack. Insert a bent piece of wire, snag the string (jiggle the string to help snag it), and pull it through. Attach the phone cable to the string with tape and pull it up through the hole above.

**4** Strip and connect wires to the terminals of a wall jack. Mount the jack to the LV ring and install the cover plate.

# GLOSSARY

For terms not included here, or for more about those that are, refer to the index on *pages 118–120.*

**Amp:** Short for ampere, this is a measurement of the strength of electrical current flowing through a wire or appliance. An amperage rating tells the greatest amount of current a wire, device, or appliance can carry.

**Antioxidant:** A paste applied to aluminum wires to inhibit corrosion and maintain safe connections.

**Armored cable:** Flexible metal sheathing containing two or more insulated wires.

**Ballast:** A transformer that regulates the voltage in a fluorescent lamp.

**Bell wire:** A thin, typically 18-gauge, wire used for doorbells.

**Box:** A metal or plastic container with openings for cable. All electrical connections must be made inside a code-approved electrical box.

**Bus bar:** A long terminal inside a service panel. Circuit breakers or fuses connect to hot bus bars; neutral and ground wires connect to neutral and grounding bus bars. Some service panels have separate bus bars for neutral and ground wires (required in Canada), while others have only one neutral/ground bus bar.

**BX:** Armored cable containing insulated wires and no ground wire; the sheathing acts as the grounding path.

**Cable:** Two or more insulated wires wrapped in metal or plastic sheathing.

**Circuit:** Also called a "branch circuit." Two or more wires carrying power from the service panel to devices, fixtures, and appliances and then back to the panel. Each circuit is protected by a circuit breaker or fuse in the service panel.

**Circuit breaker:** A protective device in a service panel that automatically shuts off power to its circuit when it senses a short circuit or overload.

**Codes:** Local regulations governing safe wiring practices. *See National Electrical Code (NEC).*

**Common terminal:** On a three-way switch, the darker-colored terminal (often marked "COM") to which the wire supplying power is connected.

**Common wire:** In a three-way switch setup, the wire that brings power to the switch or to the fixture.

**Conductor:** A carrier of electricity—usually, a wire.

**Conduit:** Plastic or metal pipe through which wires run.

**Continuity tester.** A device that tells whether a circuit is capable of carrying electricity.

**Cord:** Two or more insulated stranded wires encased in a flexible plastic or cloth sheathing.

**Current:** The flow of electrons through a conductor.

**Device:** Usually, an electrical receptacle or switch.

**Duplex receptacle:** The most common type of receptacle, with two outlets.

**Electrical Metallic Tubing (EMT):** Thin rigid metal conduit, suitable for residential use. Also called Thinwall.

**End-line wiring:** A method of wiring a switch, in which power runs first to the fixture and then to the switch.

**End-of-the-run:** A receptacle at the end of a circuit.

**Feed wire:** The hot wire that brings power into a box.

**Fixture:** A light or fan that is permanently attached, rather than being plugged into a receptacle.

**Four-way switch:** A switch used when a light is controlled by three or more switches.

**Fuse:** A safety device, located in a fuse box, which shuts off power when a circuit overloads.

**Greenfield:** Flexible metal conduit.

**Ground:** Wire or metal sheathing that provides an alternate path for current back to the service panel (and from there to a grounding rod sunk in the earth, or to a cold-water pipe). Grounding protects against shock in case of an electrical malfunction.

**Ground fault circuit interruptor (GFCI):** A receptacle with a built-in safety feature, which shuts off when there is a risk of shock.

**Hard-wired:** An appliance that is wired via cable directly into a box, rather than having a cord that plugs into a receptacle.

**Hot wire:** The wire that carries power, and is either black or colored.

**Junction box:** An electrical box with no fixture or device attached; it is used to split a circuit into different branches.

**Kilowatt (kW):** One thousand watts.

**Knockout:** A round slug or a tab that can be punched out to allow room for a cable or circuit breaker.

**LB fitting:** A pulling elbow made for outdoor use.

**Lead:** A wire (usually stranded) connected to a fixture.

**MC cable:** Armored cable with a ground wire in addition to at least two insulated wires.

**Middle-of-the-run:** A receptacle located between the service panel and another receptacle. Wires continue from its box and on to one or more other receptacle boxes.

**Multitester:** A tool that measures voltage of various levels, tests for continuity, and performs other tests.

**National Electrical Code (NEC):** The standard set of electrical codes for the United States, updated every few years. Local codes sometimes vary from the NEC.

**Neon tester:** *See* Voltage tester.

**Neutral wire:** A wire, usually covered with white insulation, that carries power from the box back to the service panel. *See also* Hot wire and Ground.

**Nonmetallic (NM) cable:** Usually, two or more insulated wires, plus a bare ground wire, enclosed in plastic sheathing. Older NM cable may have no ground wire and cloth rather than plastic sheathing.

**Old-work box:** *See* Remodel box.

**Outlet:** Any point in an electrical system where electricity may be used. Receptacles, fixtures, switches, and hard-wired appliances are all outlets.

**Overload:** A dangerous condition caused when a circuit carries more amperage than it is designed to handle. Overloaded wires overheat. A circuit breaker or fuse protects wires from overheating.

**Pigtail:** A short length of wire, spliced with two or more wires in a box and connected to a terminal, so that two or more wires will not be attached to a terminal.

**Plug:** A male connection at the end of a cord, designed to be inserted into a receptacle outlet.

**Polarized plug:** A plug with its neutral prong wider than the hot prong. It can be inserted into a receptacle outlet in only one way,

thereby insuring against reversing the hot and neutral sides of a circuit.

**Raceway:** Surface-mounted channels, made of plastic or metal, through which wires can be run to extend a circuit.

**Receptacle:** An electrical outlet into which a plug can be inserted.

**Recessed canister light:** A light fixture that contains its own electrical box, designed to be installed inside a ceiling so that its trim and perhaps lens are flush with the ceiling surface.

**Remodel box:** A metal or plastic electrical box that clamps to a wall surface (either plaster or drywall), rather than being fastened to framing. A remodel box must have an internal clamp to hold the cable.

**Rigid conduit:** Metal conduit that can be bent only with a special tool.

**Romex:** A common name for nonmetallic cable.

**Service entrance:** The point where power from the utility enters the house. A service entrance may be underground, or it may be at or near the roof.

**Service panel:** A large electrical box, containing either fuses or circuit breakers. Power from the utility enters the service panel, where it is divided up into branch circuits. Also called a panel box or main panel.

**Short circuit:** A dangerous condition that occurs when a hot wire touches a neutral wire, a ground wire, a metal box that is part of the ground system, or another hot wire.

**Splice:** To connect together the stripped ends of two or more wires, usually by twisting them together and adding a wire nut.

**Stripping:** Removing insulation from wire or sheathing from cable.

**Subpanel:** A subsidiary service panel, containing circuit breakers or fuses and supplying a number of branch circuits. A subpanel is itself controlled by the main service panel.

**System ground:** The method by which an entire electrical system is grounded; usually a thick wire leading either to one or more rods sunk deep in the earth, or to a cold-water pipe.

**Three-way switch:** A switch used when a light is controlled by two switches.

**Transformer:** A device that reduces voltage, usually from 120 volts to between 4 and 24 volts. Doorbells, thermostats, and low-voltage lights all use transformers.

**Traveler wires:** In a three-way switch setup, the two wires that run from switch to switch. *See* Common wire.

**Underwriter's knot:** A special knot used to tie the wires in a lamp socket.

**Volt (V):** A measure of electrical pressure; volts X amps = watts.

**Voltage detector:** A tool that senses electrical current, even through insulation and sheathing.

**Voltage tester:** A tool that senses the presence of electrical current when its probes touch bare wire ends. Some voltage testers (often called voltmeters) also tell how many volts are present.

**Watt (W):** A measure of the amount of power that an electrical device, fixture, or appliance uses.

**Wire nut:** A plastic protective cap that screws onto two twisted-together wires to complete a splice.

# INDEX

## METRIC CONVERSIONS

| U.S. Units to Metric Equivalents | | | Metric Units to U.S. Equivalents | | |
| --- | --- | --- | --- | --- | --- |
| To convert from | Multiply by | To get | To convert from | Multiply by | To get |
| Inches | 25.4 | Millimeters | Millimeters | 0.0394 | Inches |
| Inches | 2.54 | Centimeters | Centimeters | 0.3937 | Inches |
| Feet | 30.48 | Centimeters | Centimeters | 0.0328 | Feet |
| Feet | 0.3048 | Meters | Meters | 3.2808 | Feet |
| Yards | 0.9144 | Meters | Meters | 1.0936 | Yards |
| Square inches | 6.4516 | Square centimeters | Square centimeters | 0.1550 | Square inches |
| Square feet | 0.0929 | Square meters | Square meters | 10.764 | Square feet |
| Square yards | 0.8361 | Square meters | Square meters | 1.1960 | Square yards |
| Acres | 0.4047 | Hectares | Hectares | 2.4711 | Acres |
| Cubic inches | 16.387 | Cubic centimeters | Cubic centimeters | 0.0610 | Cubic inches |
| Cubic feet | 0.0283 | Cubic meters | Cubic meters | 35.315 | Cubic feet |
| Cubic feet | 28.316 | Liters | Liters | 0.0353 | Cubic feet |
| Cubic yards | 0.7646 | Cubic meters | Cubic meters | 1.308 | Cubic yards |
| Cubic yards | 764.55 | Liters | Liters | 0.0013 | Cubic yards |

*To convert from degrees Fahrenheit (F) to degrees Celsius (C), first subtract 32, then multiply by ⅝.*

*To convert from degrees Celsius to degrees Fahrenheit, multiply by ⅝, then add 32.*